TRANSFORM YOUR SELF

TRANSFORM YOUR SELF

Finding Stability in an Unstable World

Acharya Mahapragya

HarperCollins *Publishers* India
a joint venture with
THE
INDIA
TODAY
GROUP

New Delhi

First published in India in 2011 by
HarperCollins *Publishers* India
a joint venture with
The India Today Group

Copyright © Jain Vishva Bharati 2011

ISBN: 978-93-5029-114-6

2 4 6 8 10 9 7 5 3 1

HarperCollins *Publishers*
A-53, Sector 57, Noida, Uttar Pradesh 201301, India
77-85 Fulham Palace Road, London W6 8JB, United Kingdom
Hazelton Lanes, 55 Avenue Road, Suite 2900, Toronto, Ontario M5R 3L2
and 1995 Markham Road, Scarborough, Ontario M1B 5M8, Canada
25 Ryde Road, Pymble, Sydney, NSW 2073, Australia
31 View Road, Glenfield, Auckland 10, New Zealand
10 East 53rd Street, New York NY 10022, USA

Typeset in 10.5/15 ITC Giovanni Std
InoSoft Systems

Printed and bound at
Manipal Technologies Limited, Manipal.

Contents

CONTENTS

Preface

The body, mind and *chitta* (psyche) are closely interrelated. The body is a special structure composed of physical atoms. The mind is a more subtle atomic structure. The chitta is a conscious ray, which works with our body and mind. The chitta is incorporeal in nature, it does not have any colour or physical properties. The body and mind are physical or material – they have colour, smell, taste and touch.

While the body and mind are both physical, the chitta is metaphysical. Yet both attributes have a parallel influence on each other. Of the four characteristics of matter – colour, smell, taste and touch – colour has the strongest influence on the chitta. Our chitta is active in our nervous system and its nucleus is the brain. The chitta is associated with consciousness in the inner world, which directs and instructs it. At the external level, the chitta reflects energy in the form of the aura, a circular envelope of rays that covers our body. The aura is the mirror image of the chitta. Each is identified through the other. Pure chitta leads to a pure aura and impure chitta leads to an impure aura.

The structure of our aura depends on our emotions. It changes constantly. Purity and impurity, expansion and contraction – these are all different states of aura. One can detect the change in consciousness through the change in aura. Physical and psychological modes can also be detected through the aura. Before affecting the physical body any disease appears in the micro body. Then the micro body reflects its image at the level of aura. Therefore, by studying the aura, any incident that is going to happen in the future can also be predicted. Many facets of life – like disease, death, health and attitude – can be predicted through the aura.

The aura changes according to one's *leshya* or emotions. Conversely, by transforming the aura through colour meditation, one can alter the leshya as well. For this reason, *leshya dhyan* or colour meditation is significant. Our thinking pattern, body postures, body motions and body movements pursue our leshya. A man in an aggressive posture is more likely to get angry. One who has the emotions of forgiveness finds it easier to stay in the consciousness of forgiveness.

There is a growing interest in books on meditation. Readers often use such books as guides to the practice of meditation. This is a positive trend and will contribute to the widespread practice of meditation. It is my wish that everyone seeks to develop his latent spirituality. I hope that each individual will learn to recognize his or her existence and potential for inner peace and higher consciousness.

Last, but certainly not least, I bow down to my Guru, Acharya Tulsi for his guidance, to all humanity.

Acharya Mahapragya

1
Manifestations of Personality

Man has many psyches. He embodies multiple possibilities of consciousness.
A man in the morning cannot be identified as the same man at noon. How
frequently the personality keeps changing! How constantly the forms change!

It is very hard to understand the variations of personality. A man who was calm and quiet in the morning might become as hot as the scorching sun at noon, just as the ocean, so quiet at dawn, is full of turbulent waves during high tide. The ocean gets lost during the changing tide. In the same way, when a person's thoughts and emotions are turbulent, his humanity is lost. As the saying goes: *Aneg-citte khalu ayam purise*, a man is multi-minded.

Everyone has multiple psyches within himself, and these psyches change constantly – with place, time and situations. But a man's personality has more facets than a magician has tricks. When the mind is changed, everything around it changes, both in the internal and external worlds. Both worlds, like the waves of an ocean, are shaken; both vibrate.

It is not in man's nature to behave badly. Nobody chooses to have polluted thoughts, negative emotions or evil actions. But these take place constantly. We believe that if someone chooses to carry out negative deeds it is natural and acceptable. It can then be maintained that he did what he wanted in accordance with his nature. But the truth is that actions and thoughts do not always follow one's inner desires.

Over time, the actions of a man will include both good and bad behaviour. These two contradictory states go hand in hand within the same person. Why is this? Why is our mind in a state of constant flux? Why are our emotions not stable? Why does our thinking pattern not remain the same? For centuries, man has pursued the answer to this dilemma. Various schools of science and mind have tried to understand this phenomenon. Psychologists have also attempted to resolve this matter, but their research is limited or incomplete. There is room to expand our knowledge in a deeper, more substantive way.

There are three human attributes in which further study is helpful in understanding the personality: the senses, the mind and the intellect. Our human 'personality component' has no other attributes that we – so far – can identify.

In today's scientific world, every organ of our body, both major and microscopic, has been scrutinized by physicians. Doctors understand the inner workings of our heart, brain, intestines, kidneys, nerves and microscopic organs. But the world of knowledge does not end with an understanding of the physical, by internalizing through our eyes, through the fickleness of our mind or through our wavering intellect. There is another process of knowing where our physical eyes do not work. In this process, the eyes are closed, the mind is shut down and the intellect is inactive. The state of being we attain or experience during this process is amazing;

it is a completely new experience that cannot be achieved by any physical means.

Our body consists of aggregates, comprising infinite atoms. When we speak we need atoms of speech, which exist within us and are spread around us. At first they are beyond our experience, but as soon as we decide to speak, these atoms of speech take the shape of words. After this, they manifest themselves as comprehensible sounds in the form of words and move into the arena of space to be acquired and understood. This is how the phenomenon of speech works. Prior to speech, there is one more phenomenon: thought. Thoughts are the precursor to speech. Therefore, ideally, everybody thinks before speaking. There are atoms of thought which help us think. Without their help, the process of thinking is not achievable. These thought-atoms are all-pervading. How do we attract these atoms?

It is human nature to determine or desire the intended activity before carrying it out. Therefore, we desire thought before we actually think. There is a very small time-frame between the determination of thinking and the activity of thinking so normally we do not notice this gap. But it exists. After determination of thinking, thought-atoms get attracted by our consciousness and take the shape of our thinking pattern. Immediately after, these shapes are spread throughout space. All of us are surrounded by atoms, which include atoms of speech, atoms of thought, atoms of emotion, atoms of colour, and many more. We do not perceive them; we do not know them. Our eyes are restricted to seeing gross or material things only, because the eyes themselves are gross. It is a simple law that gross means can lead to gross ends. Fortunately, this is good. If our eyes could see the subtle objects, the visible world would have been over-crowded and the eyes would confuse the brain about how to discern what it sees and doesn't see. So this limitation of the extent of our physical capacities works in our favour.

The subtle or micro world is neither the subject of sense organs, nor the subject of mind and intellect. To get into the subtle world, we do not use these three systems. Give up the sense organs, give up the mind, and give up the intellect. Shut down all the systems because these three systems take us to the external world. When these are left behind our internal journey begins. This internal journey helps us understand the subtle world and its hidden treasures. Great leaders gave us the solution by illuminating their internal journeys for us. But to understand the best direction for this journey we must first understand the function of the inner world.

Man is very bad at maintaining the conviction of his personal resolutions. He makes personal vows or commitments – for instance, that he will never think or act negatively – but his resolution breaks down. Why does he do this? If we try to understand personality beyond a superficial level, we can see the two oceans existing within every personality. One is the ocean of negativity, the other is the ocean of positivity. They are extremely large and they constantly vibrate and flow. The two types of energy flow are positive (benevolent) and negative (malevolent). When negative energy flows, man is compelled to think and act negatively. Though he does not wish to do so, his senses and muscles perform unwanted acts. Is man at fault for this? Not at all. It is the fault of the malevolent stream that compels us to think negatively, leads to negative emotions and compels our body towards negative actions.

On the other hand, when the stream of benevolent energy is active, good thoughts, good emotions and good behaviour all come into effect, whether or not we want them. This means man is not responsible for his deeds and thoughts. The source and the inertia are hidden within the self. The two streams of positive and negative energy compel us to act in accordance with the dominant energy flow of the moment.

> Our personality is the reflection of our inner stream. The actions of man are a consequence of his internal energy; he does not have independent choice. But can we say that we hold no responsibility for our deeds because they are beyond our control? Of course not! Such things cannot abdicate us of our responsibility for our good or bad deeds.

If we think deeply we begin to raise questions. Why does positive energy come from inside? Why does our inner world give off negative energy? Why does energy vacillate between positive and negative? Why do we have two quite different natures? We have to figure out the solution. Let us take an example. Suppose there is a big canal with two gates. When the gates are open, water starts flowing through the gap. If the gates are shut, water cannot pass through. Similarly, when we open the door of negative energy it starts flowing out, and when we open the door of positive energy, positivity begins to flow. The next question is, who opens the door? It is our own 'self' that opens the door of negative or positive energy. There is nothing beyond the 'self' or 'me'. Sometimes we open the door of positive energy and shut the other one, and sometimes we open the door of negative energy and shut the positive one. Only one door is open at a time. Consequently, there is no doubt that the self is responsible for all good and bad manifestations, whether these are thoughts, emotions or actions. And the one with the key to the door holds the key to the root of responsibility.

We have two keys in this realm of consciousness – one key to open the door of negativity and another to open the door of positivity. We might want to use the keys to lock the door of negativity for ever and unlock the door of positive energy. If such a thing could happen, it would be an amazing experience. We would no longer be burdened with negative thoughts, emotions or actions. We might be eager to make this happen and such excitement is natural.

We will have to be very careful; make sure we have not exchanged the keys. We have two keys and two locks. When we use the key of delusion, the door of negativity opens and we are inundated with negative emotions, thoughts and deeds which we cannot get rid of until the door is closed. The second key is awareness. When the key of awareness is utilized, the world of positive energy is unlocked, which brings with it unbounded goodness. The key to awareness works in two ways – it opens the lock of the positive world and at the same time locks away the negative world. When this key of awareness is at our disposal, the inner world of consciousness is awakened, which emanates pure thought, pure emotion and pure conduct.

How do we get the key? Even if the key is in our hand and we know it can assist us in awakening our consciousness, we must know how to turn it. The simplest and most important way is to be aware of our breathing. If we are aware of our breathing, we are aware of our mind. And if we are aware of our mind, our consciousness is awakened. This state of awareness is the key to opening the world of pure, positive and higher consciousness.

The second way to turn the key is through perception of the body. If we are not aware of our body, the body within which the key is placed and stimulated, we cannot turn the key to unlock the door of positive energy. You may wonder why we need to be aware of our body. How does perception of the body facilitate the course of action? Our body is like a screen. All our emotional waves – whether anger, greed or ego – are displayed through the body. In our body, the nervous system helps to display the emotions at the physical level.

Suppose you are sitting quietly. Suddenly you get angry for some reason. As soon as the emotion of anger is active the very thoughts of anger start rising at the mental level. The anger does not actually 'come alive' until it rides along the nerves. Internally, the anger might be very intense, but if the neural network does not help, anger will not manifest itself in the body. Therefore, the nervous system sends the message through the nerves to the corresponding body parts to show the anger. For example, the face and eyes turn red, the muscles become tensed. This is how anger is expressed at the physical level. Otherwise anger would dissipate at the mental level.

Perception of the body is, therefore, very significant. If you perceive your body, you become aware of the thousands of sensitive centres in the body. These vital centres are the nexus of exchanging energy and our personality is expressed through them. Each emotion has its own centre of manifestation. So there is a certain place for anger in your body. When you get angry, your body is provoked and an energy of the corresponding frequency hits a particular part of the body where anger gets converted into sensation. Your eyes become red, your lips begin to throb and your tone changes. If you are aware of your body and able to control your nerves, then the emotions will not have a platform to reveal themselves. Thus you are able to subside or pacify your anger.

Our objective is to erase negative emotions. Subsiding only controls the emotions. If emotions are not destroyed, they remain dormant. Subsiding emotions has its own value. It is the first step to destruction. Until we learn to appease, until we learn to control our emotions, it is difficult to destroy them. For example, when you fall sick, you first attempt to control the effects of the disease. Then you begin treatment to eliminate the disease from the root. Eliminating or uprooting is a long-term process. So, if someone were suffering from a severe, unbearable pain and was faced with the option of long-term treatment to uproot the disease without controlling the pain, he would be unlikely to choose this option. The patient would rather control the pain first and then uproot the disease. In the same way, control is the first step to uprooting the disease of negative emotions.

Perception awakens the nervous system. This is significant. The power of the nervous system defines the power of man. Strong muscles and bones are not enough to make a man powerful. If you can awaken your nervous system through perception of your body, so that it follows your instructions and controls the negative emotions within, then your emotions cannot dominate you and they do not get manifested.

For practising perception of body we first need to understand the body. An emotional impulse manifests itself at three different levels – mind, body and speech. For example, a man gets angry. At the muscular or physical level, his eyes and face express his rage or he might react violently . At the mental level, he thinks negatively. At the verbal level, he speaks aggressively. These three levels work independently. But the question is: are they really three different systems or is there only one system that manifests emotions externally?

In the age of Lord Mahavir and Lord Buddha, one question was repeatedly asked: How many types of violence or negative activity can we truly identify?

Lord Mahavir said, 'Violence is three-fold: mental, verbal and physical.'

Lord Buddha said, 'Violence is only one-fold: mental. Neither verbal nor physical holds any place; only mental violence takes place.'

Many scholars have stated that the mind is the only cause of bondage and liberation, the cause of impurity and purity. They think that the mind both binds us and determines our freedom. Most people believe that our mind is responsible for every move, activity, behaviour and attitude. This idea is true but incomplete. The three-fold concept of violence or negativity put forward by Lord Mahavir is a scientific approach. Let's analyse the independent function of each of the three levels of manifestation of emotions. Until we know these levels we cannot stop negativity and the practice of perception of the body is impossible.

Let's first consider the physical or muscular level. Often, our body gets used to something and demands it again and again, whether or not the mind wants it. For example, a person who is addicted to alcohol and wants to quit the habit still feels the urge to drink. Or a person might commit a negative act under the influence of his peers. We often decide that we will not show our anger but when the time comes, we lose control. Our actions do not follow our thoughts. When the nervous system receives an impression from the inner world, the impression takes on a reality. Our mind freezes and our body becomes a place for the prominent exhibition of emotions. Thus, there are many areas where our mind does not have control over our actions. In this case the negativity must be controlled at the physical level.

Similarly, at the mental level you might think of cheating someone, but your body does not necessarily show this. Here, the mind has an independent function; the body is not involved.

We often say things we do not mean; the words just slip out. This implies that our vocal system is not led by our thoughts. This is because we have programmed our muscles in such a way that it is hard for them to stop. So we can say that all three levels – physical, mental and verbal – function independently to manifest the emotions.

We need to understand that the mind does not drive our verbal or physical attitude – our emotions do.

Each of the three systems has its own *pran* or vital energy to function. In Jain philosophy, pran is ten-fold. Five of them vitalize the five sense organs. One pran is associated with each – mind, body and speech. One pran gives energy for breathing and one keeps our life charged.

Mental bio-potentiality helps the mind function. Verbal and physical pran help speech and body respectively. So the three levels need separate energies to work.

The impulses within us first get connected with the nervous system. Then, according to the quality of the impulse, the nervous system sends a message to the brain for thought or to the vocal cords for speech or to different muscles for physical action. When your desires and stimulations travel through your nervous system, things happen of their own accord, irrespective of your intentions. The mind does not have control over the nervous system. The mind, speech and the body have their own separate sub-systems, each with its own significance. One attribute cannot be considered to have a higher value than the others. Therefore, to stop negative attitudes at the external level, we first have to control the mind, body and speech.

The body transmits negative signals from the external to the internal world. Malevolent energies are attracted to the body by any negative activity of our mind, body or speech. The negative energy is transmitted through a specific process which I will discuss in a later chapter. There are two worlds inside our bodies – internal and external. The internal is the world of the consciousness or soul which is contaminated by malevolent energy.

Each living organism has a soul that gives him life. When the soul leaves the body, the same body remains but it is worthless. The body, mind and speech function only in the presence of the soul. The soul is pure in itself, but attracts harmful atoms due to negative emotions like anger, ego, violence, and jealousy. These atoms are known as 'karma' in Jain philosophy. Karma conceals the pure nature and contaminates the soul. Each soul carries the accumulated karma into its next life. In each life we shed karma by doing righteous activity and acquire more karma with evil actions.

> You see a new model of car. You immediately want to possess it. As a result of this desire, you attract karma, because greed is a negative emotion. Karma covers and pollutes the soul. This union of soul with karma is your inner world. Later, this karmic energy is sent to the emotional world, which forces you to crave again. The emotional or external world within you is what draws you to material objects and connects you with the world outside you. Of course, the body helps in this entire process.

The body keeps accumulating an influx of negative emotions from its surroundings. Over time, this accumulation increases and creates a vast internal world. The body helps to create this world by accommodating the external streams. We can also say that the body, like speech, is responsible for both bondage and liberation. In other words, positive thinking, speech and action lead to liberation while negative thinking, speech and action lead to bondage.

When you are aware of your body, you may be able to address the negative emotions of delusion and other, more damaging desires. Thus, you gain control of your nervous system and can transform the world of negative emotions into a positive one. You can be in control. In this state, deceit, greed and every other negative stream is blocked, stopped or restricted. You have mastered the key to controlling them. And once you know how to control negative emotions, you can drive them out; you can uproot them all the way.

This is how *preksha* or perception works. You can understand preksha by understanding the process of perception of the body.

By becoming aware of your body, you can stop the outflow of malevolent energy from within, by controlling and then eliminating it. Thus you can attain the state of purity.

PERCEPTION OF THE BODY: HOW TO PRACTISE

1. Sit in a comfortable posture.
2. *Gyan mudra:* Put your hands on your knees, palms turned up. Touch the tip of your index finger to the tip of your thumb. Let the other fingers remain straight.
3. Gently close your eyes.
4. *Mahapran dhwani:* Concentrate your mind on your brain. Breathe in through your nostrils, and while exhaling make a resonant humming sound through your nose, like a buzzing bee. Practise 9 times.
5. Focus your mind on the big toe of your right foot for about 5 seconds. Perceive and experience the vibrations and sensations taking place in this part of your body. Then, focus your consciousness to the other parts of your right leg, one by one.
6. Similarly experience the vibrations of your entire left leg, torso, hips, shoulder, front and back; right and left hand; neck, the different parts of your face, head and brain. Concentrate on each organ for 5 seconds.
7. After this, allow your mind a quick trip from your toes to your head and back. Experience every sensation, pain or pleasure.
8. Now undertake the slow journey over your whole body once again.
9. Conclude the practice with three long breaths.

PROGRESSIVE STAGES OF PERCEPTION OF BODY

Experience of superficial sensations of the skin, cloth, warmth, perspiration, itchiness, tingling and others.

↓

Experience of sensations produced by muscular movement.

↓

Experience of sensations produced by the functioning of internal organs such as the heart, liver, lungs and others.

↓

Experience of subtle vibrations produced by the electrical impulses travelling within the nervous system and the flow of vital energy in the body. This last is the true perception of the body.

ESSENCE

❖ Man has multiple facets to his personality.

❖ Actions can be good, bad or stagnant.

❖ Sometimes thoughts are positive, at other times negative. There is also a state that is void of thought.

❖ A person can feel positive or negative emotions – or even be emotionless.

❖ An individual can feel love/hate; attachment/aversion; desire/ detachment.

❖ Emotional states can range from trust to doubt, humour to fear, openness to deceit.

❖ Man does not like bad actions, bad thoughts and evil emotions, yet he indulges in evil. Why?

❖ Man has a big pool within and two streams incessantly flow out of it:

    a) Flow of positive energy

    b) Flow of negative energy

❖ By the electric force of vital energy they are forced to flow from outside to inside.

❖ Our delusion opens the door of negative energy.

2
Structure of Personality
CONNECTING POINT OF SOUL AND BODY

Adhyavasay is found in all living forms and it is this which connects the soul with the physical self. Why are plants sensitive even if they do not have a mind? It is because of adhyavasay. In plants, adhyavasay is directly transformed into sensation. Therefore, plants have the capacity of recognition, memory and understanding others' feelings.

The universe is comprised of two entities – soul and non-soul; one entity contains life and the other is non-living or lifeless. The living being is conscious while the non-living body is without consciousness.

Some schools of philosophy in the west and the *charvak* philosophy in India accept only the physical or non-living self as what is real. They deny the very existence of the soul. But there are other philosophies that propose a completely different dynamic: that the soul has an independent existence. How do we account for these two fundamentally different schools of thought?

Those who accept that the mind contains all known reality do not acknowledge that consciousness extends beyond what we physically perceive. They reject any theory of consciousness beyond their personal understanding, which is limited at best.

Fortunately, those who do not limit their acceptance of reality to the corporeal have a wider understanding of consciousness. There are two forces at work in this paradigm: adhyavasay (conscious energy or prime drives) and chitta (psyche or conscious mind). The chitta, though conscious in nature, addresses the corporeal or physical body, whereas adhyavasay extends consciousness beyond the body. Adhyavasay is the field of conscious vibrations working with karmic energy. Pure conscious vibrations from the soul cross the field of *kashay* or passion, After coming out, the vibrations affected by the kashay form a field, which is called adhyavasay. When our conscious energy ascends to adhyavasay, our body is left behind.

Kashay is the impulse of delusion which stains the consciousness with its own colour. In other words, kashay is a malevolent energy because of attachment and aversion. It is four-fold, consisting of anger, ego, deceit and greed. Whenever any activity is done at the physical, mental or verbal level, biased by attachment or aversion, the soul attracts inauspicious karma. This karma forms the field of kashay, stays there for a certain time and then is shed.

There are two stages of karma:

1. Rising
2. Cessation

Rising karma leaves its effect on the conscious vibrations passing through this field. In this case, the adhyavasay also becomes malevolent and hence its manifestation at the physical level is harmful.

Cessation is three-fold: subsidence, subsidence-cum-destruction and total destruction. In all three stages karma is ineffective. If there is cessation of karma in any form, the conscious vibrations passing through the field of kashay do not get affected and hence stay pure. Consequently, the adhyavsay is pure and at the physical level the thought, attitude or behaviour is also pure.

Adhyavasay, being subtle in nature, is beyond the perception of common man, but it connects the soul and body.

Spiritual leaders consider the body and soul to be two distinct entities. But if they are different, how are they related? What is the point where the body and consciousness come together? This is a complex question that must consider the physical, the spiritual and the many points of understanding in-between.

Let's approach this a little differently. The soul is the nucleus, the centre, which is conscious. This is surrounded by the field of kashay, which is harmful to the soul. The latter is so powerful it rules over the soul.

As a matter of fact, the soul is potentially the most powerful because it is pure, but kashay becomes more powerful and dominates the soul, hiding its purity. So, the pure conscious energy always has to pass through the domain of impure kashay.

From the kashay, the conscious energy enters the next orbit, the field of adhyavasay. This system works actively with *taijas sharir* or the bioelectric body. The taijas sharir gives energy to the field of adhyavasay. Adhyavasay is more important than the mind. It is not your mind that makes you good or evil, positive or negative, pure or impure; it is adhyavasay. A lay person cannot understand this. Only one who has realized himself can estimate the value of adhyavasay. Adhyavasay is the point where the consciousness and body can be experienced separately and the relation between the two can be understood. In mundane life and worldly activities it is hard to experience the existence of adhyavasay, whereas the mind is easy to recognize. That is why the mind is easily accepted.

The domain of the mind is unique. The mind is not found in every living being; it exists only in human beings and in intellectually-developed animals. Adhyavasay, on the other hand, is found in all living beings, including plants.

It is believed that all living beings – from one-sensed beings like plants to five-sensed beings like humans – are subject to the bonds of karma. A being with a mind certainly attracts karma, but so do living beings without a mind. In *Sutrakritang*, the second canonical text of Jainism, Mahavir explains this in a very interesting way: When active the mundane soul attracts karma because of its actions. When one goes to sleep at night, the conscious mind is inactive. The person is in such deep sleep that he cannot even dream, yet he is attracting and bonding karma. This is important because it is believed that only an active state of mind is responsible for bonding karma. But here we see that even when you are in a deep and dreamless sleep, where conscious activity is impossible, karma enters the body. And if a person has perverse visions or wrong perspectives, he is attracting negative karma in the form of any one of the eighteen sins described in Jainism.

When Mahavir's disciple heard this, he asked, 'Lord, how is it possible that a sleeping man can draw karma?' Lord Mahavir explained this with two examples.

The first example is more significant as it explains the whole idea of adhyavasay. A plant has life but neither mind nor speech. It only has a body, which is in a constant state of sleep. The consciousness of such an existence is forever dormant. Plants do not possess mental faculties yet they attract the eighteen negative karma. How does this happen? Lord Mahavir explained that this happens through the adhyavasay, as plants have innumerable expressions of adhyavasay. The expressions of adhyavasay may be benevolent or malevolent. Malevolent expression – actions of violence, possessiveness, anger, greed, pride, deceit and the like – is responsible for karmic bondage, and plants possess all these negative expressions and emotions. These beings do not have a mind or speech, but they do have instincts, feelings and sensations, which cause them to unite with karma.

Based on our knowledge of the physical, the brain, mind and speech hold the highest places in the context of knowledge. But the greatest source of knowledge in the subtle world is adhyavasay. According to physical science, the cell is the smallest unit that helps us to know. Cells deliver the same knowledge transmitted by adhyavasay. The lowest life forms, which have neither mind nor brain, know the world through cells. Science postulates that the cells in plants are more sensitive than those in human beings. Why are plants more sensitive if they do not have a mind? It is because of adhyavasay. In plants, adhyavasay is directly transformed into sensations, so they are more likely to have the capacity of recognition, memory and understanding others' feelings.

A well-known scientist, Dr Cleve Backster, has performed a number of experiments on the subtle behaviour of plants. One experiment was particularly telling in its outcome.

The experiment began with two plants located in an empty room, six volunteer participants and one sheet of paper. He divided the paper into six pieces. On one of the pieces he wrote: 'One of the two plants in the room will be pulled from its pot and crushed.' The remaining five were left blank. He then separately folded all six pieces of paper, put them on the table and left the room.

Next, he put a blindfold over the eyes of the six volunteers before they entered the room. They were each told to pick up one of the folded papers and asked to follow the instructions on the paper (if there were any). None of them knew what was written on the sheets.

The volunteer who had picked up the paper with the written statement followed through as instructed. He pulled one of the plants out of the pot from its roots and began to rip it apart. Afterwards, all the participants left the room.

Then a polygraph machine was connected to the remaining plant. Dr Backster asked the six participants to re-enter the room. He was, to this point, unaware which person had uprooted the plant. Each participant was asked to stand briefly next to the remaining plant to see if there was any detectable reaction from the plant. Five of the volunteers stood next to the plant without eliciting a response detectable by the polygraph. However, as the last person approached the plant, a very noticeable response was detected by the polygraph, substantially different from the other responses. The plant recognized that this person had destroyed the other plant and was frightened of him. This proves that plants have intuitive attributes that are not available or readily accessible to humans.

Dr Backster performed a second experiment with other plants. Again, a polygraph machine was connected to a number of plants. While he was in the room with the plants, he thought of setting fire to the plants. As soon as he focused on this thought, the pointer of the polygraph started to move. The pointer was showing the apprehension of the plants based on his thoughts. As long as he kept thinking the same thought, the polygraph indicated the fear experienced by the plants. He got up and went outside. Abruptly, he changed his mind and returned to the room with a positive feeling and moved close to the plants with the thought of not hurting them. The effect was amazing. There was no movement in the pointer. The plants were at ease.

Men cannot read each other's minds but plants seem to do so – how do we explain this? What helps plants sense so strongly? It seems that there are attributes of knowing that are beyond the abilities of the mind. The mind is not the foundation or source of knowledge. The source of knowledge is adhyavasay. It is the origin of all sensation. Man approaches this understanding from the opposite direction, ignoring the adhyavasay and viewing the mind as the source of all knowledge.

The soul or consciousness is at the centre, surrounded by the field of kashay. The field of adhyavasay or conscious energy is next. Till this level, the physical body has no function. Only the karmic body and taijas sharir have control over these fields.

The karmic and bioelectric bodies have no limbs, neurological network or brain. There is no spinal cord. There is not a single means to a centre of knowledge. Yet they are capable of cognition. You might wonder what the significance of such bodies is. These subtle bodies have knowledge, not in a sentient sense, but through adhyavasay.

Since adhyavasay has conscious power, it has the potential to know. This knowledge does not require organs or physical faculties. It can access knowledge without the help of the physical body and is the border between physical and non-physical functioning. After this field, knowledge through the physical body comes into effect.

When impulses or vibrations come out of the field of adhyavasay, they enter the domain of the corporeal. When impulses appear at the physical level, the physical body gets connected with the soul.

This means the vibrations inside start getting sensed at the physical level. The main work of conscious vibrations is the formation of chitta. Chitta, the representative of the self or consciousness, is the bridge between the physical body and the soul. It controls all mental, physical and vocal actions. The chitta is created with the help of the brain. At this level, knowledge is manifested through the organs of the physical body. Here, of course, knowledge needs the functionality of the body for its reflection. The chitta enables true knowledge of an object.

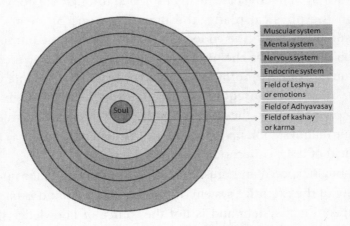

Muscular system
Mental system
Nervous system
Endocrine system
Field of Leshya or emotions
Field of Adhyavasay
Field of kashay or karma
Soul

THE VARIOUS FIELDS FROM SOUL TO BODY

Adhyavasay projects radiations which move outward in every direction. Therefore, it is said that adhyavasay has innumerable centres. The number of atoms in the adhyavasay is equal to the number of points in space. Thereafter, these ripples of impulses enter the domain of chitta, where they flow like an electromagnetic wave of impulses and enter the domain of leshya.

Leshya, literally meaning 'colour', is a technical term in Jain philosophy. It is the expression or flow of karma. The leshya is dominated by karma and endowed with certain colours, depending on the past deeds being projected. This is where incoming waves interact with the colour atoms, resulting in instincts and impulses. All impulses – both good and bad – originate in the field of leshya. Cessation of karma leads to good impulses and rising karma begets negative impulses. In other words, we can say that electro-magnetic waves are coloured as they are affected by karma. Now, the adhyavasay interacts with the endocrine system in the form of ultra-microwaves. The compulsive forces produced by the interaction of adhyavasay and leshya are finally projected through the body.

On the physical plane, the manifestations of karma are transmitted through the endocrine system. That is, the output of karma is through the chemical messengers we know as hormones. The quality of these hormones is in accordance with the intensity of past karma. Consequently, karmic expression, through the hormones, controls the physical body. The brain has no role in karmic manifestation up to this point. The field of adhyavasay and the field of leshya affect our operational system.

Thought, speech and muscular action combine to make up the faculty of the executive system. It implies that the mind is part of an operational system and is not the source of knowledge. The mind is not responsible for attracting karma nor is it capable of destroying karma. It merely follows instructions as issued from within the self. Speech too executes the instructions initiated from within. Similarly, the body is not to blame for attracting karma. These three bodily components – mind, body and speech – are responsible for physical and mental action or execution, but not simply for the sake of knowledge itself. The domain of knowledge ends at the domain of chitta and the domain of emotion ends with the domain of leshya.

Then how do knowledge and emotions move forward and get manifested at the physical level? They have modalities of expression which manifest on the physical plane, through the mind, speech and body. The function of the mind is to recall (past), to think (present) and to imagine (future). In the world of science and technology, these are seemingly mundane processes. These functions can be crudely emulated by robots and computers. What, then, is the utility of the mind? More importantly, is there a substantial difference between the mind and a computer? I think there is not much difference between the two.

A computer works in much the same way as the physical mind (the brain). So, to an extent, the mind and the computer hold equal standing – the critical distinction is the difference in the creator of each. The mind is the creation of the karmic body; the computer is the creation of man. The karmic body is an all-powerful and supremely intelligent entity which could fabricate the micro-parts of the physical body. The creative genius of man pales in comparison with his ability to replicate the abilities of the ultra-micro body. Man has been the architect of many physical marvels, but he can never be an architect of the human body. Nor has he or will he design and build a system as complicated as the neural network wonder known as the brain.

It is true that a computer can memorize and save vast amounts of information. It can serve many functions: it can solve mathematical problems and extrapolate conclusions from the input of random interrelated data just as the brain does. If you focus only on the capabilities of the mind, then there is no difference between the mind and a computer.

Let us analyse this differently. The mind is part of an executive system of sorts. It cannot be categorized as good or bad. The owner or master is responsible for the good and the bad as it is he who initiates the process. When the mind is signalled to process information, it does so. It is not responsible for the quality of the outcome. Unfortunately, the mind is deemed as the centre of any outcome, because it is the functionary, while the owners, the adhyavasay and chitta, remain obscure. The mind has to face the reaction like the ambassador to a king, the victim of anger if he delivers an unfavourable message.

Recapitulate the entire idea: consciousness or the self-forming nucleus of the living organism is at the centre, surrounded by the contaminated orbit of kashay; at the external level the outermost orbit is *yog* (mind, body and speech).

The mind is never static or constant; it goes into action as directed by the individual. The mind is a product of the processes of the individual. In fact, if you attract the atoms of thought to the mind, you are procreating the mind. If you do not wish to attract these atoms to the mind, the mind and its thinking processes will not come into effect. You will be in a thoughtless state. The activation of speech works in the same way.

The body works differently. The body is ready to act as soon as it is connected to the conscious self. Ultimately, it is up to you to initiate thoughts or actions. The potentiality of action is there, but its execution depends on your will. Go deep into yourself and understand the underlying secret.

The secret is to be aware. Be aware of your mind, your speech and your body to keep them away from external influence. This awareness will not allow any external situation to dominate the self, thus enabling a healthy execution of our mental and physical processes. If the execution system is healthy, it can deny any negative instructions that might arise.

For example, sometimes the master has to do favours for the employee in order to keep him happy and to get the work done properly. In the same manner, keep your execution system under your control. Make sure the execution system does not have control of the adhyavasay and you will reach the first step towards purity: the process of controlling negative energy.

The process of eliminating karmic energy is quite different from that of controlling it. We will discuss that later. For now, let's consider the process of control. There are three steps: perception of breathing, perception of the physical body and perception of psychic colours. Colours are very important. We do colour meditation to attract the positive colours from the cosmos and to develop purity.

First, make your mind, body and speech positive. By following negative instructions over and over, mind, body and speech have become habituated to being negative. It is a natural phenomenon. When a person gets angry, his eyebrows are knitted together, his eyes turn red, his lips start to quiver and his body begins to shake. Some people are good at feigning anger. Even in the absence of anger they pretend to be angry, and often the physical expression of anger allows the emotion to come up in our thoughts.

A play was being performed in an auditorium. It was in full flow, captivating the audience with its realistic overtones. Everything was running smoothly. Suddenly, someone from the audience walked up to the stage and slapped the actor who was playing the villain. The cast and the audience were both taken by surprise. The actor who was assaulted said, 'Sir, what are you doing? I am not bad in real life. I am merely an actor performing in a play.' The gentleman realized his mistake and apologized at once. He said, 'I am sorry. I was so engrossed in the play that I forgot you were acting. I thought you were misbehaving and could not control myself.'

Man falls prey to the weakness of an emotional reaction. This is how our body and nerves coordinate with each other. When anger rises, the body flows with it and when the body shows aggressive signals, anger overrides the nerves.

The very first step is to pay attention to the habits of the nerves, the mind and speech. If these are weak enough to be dominated by external influences, work on controlling them, changing the habit and freeing them of all outer influences.

The second step is to keep your mind, body and speech away from inner instruction. Do not let the instruction reach them. Destroy the emotional desire to respond before these emotions meet your executive system.

When these two processes – the process of controlling and the process of eliminating – work together with your other spiritual practices, the spiritual journey is uplifted and you will be successful in achieving your goal.

ESSENCE

❖ Spiritual leaders consider the body and soul to be two distinct entities.

❖ What is the relation between body and soul? The soul is at the centre surrounded by the ultra-micro body, karma. Taijas sharir provides pran or vital energy.

❖ There is no connection between the physical body and vibrations of soul in the field of adhyavasay. The vibrations of the soul are connected with karma and taijas sharir. This field of adhyavasay is where the consciousness and body can be experienced separately and the relation between the two can be understood.

❖ The vibrations of the soul go beyond the field of adhyavasay and enter the field of leshya. From here, they communicate with the physical body through the endocrine glands.

❖ The executive system consists of the mind, body and speech and works through the nervous system.

❖ Taijas sharir helps us visualize colours in meditation.

3

Control Centre of Good and Evil

The body is as neat and clean as a mirror, it reflects your thoughts and emotions without the slightest deviation. Your emotions reflect the hidden force behind the body. These reflections can take you far away and let you perceive the unknown world which is seemingly out of your reach.

Your body is like a mirror that reflects your thoughts and emotions. Your expressions reflect the underlying emotions. Sometimes you can look into a person's eyes and sense his hatred through the glare in his eyes. Even if he does not say a word, you still know his feelings through his body language, particularly through his eyes. His eyes reflect the energy of hate and no verbal communication is necessary.

Let's take another example. You look into someone's eyes and feel some force of attraction. You find the person full of love for you. His eyes draw you into his emotional world. You understand the unspoken.

The body works like a screen. Emotions do not originate at the physical level. They are produced in the subtle world and then manifested in the body. To have access to its source and further beyond its source to the pure consciousness, we must take a reverse trip from the physical to the mental, from the external to the internal world. Let us start our journey with the physical body, then penetrate within, leaving the body behind and moving forward into the subtle world – through the field of emotions, the field of leshya, the field of adhyavasay and the field of kashay, until we reach the pure soul or pure consciousness.

The field of kashay, which surrounds the soul, is significant and plays the game of emotions. Kashay or *karma sharir* (ultra-micro body) consists only of waves of energy. There are no emotions, no feelings; only vibrations. There are two types of vibrations:

1.   the vibrations of pure self
2.   the vibrations of kashay

The vibrations of pure self come from the ocean of pure consciousness and the vibrations of kashay exist in the sea of kashay. When the vibrations of pure self come out of their field and enter the field of kashay, they get influenced by the kashay and then the waves enter the adhyavasay. Until this point, the waves maintain their form of vibrations. The adhyavasay does not have any direct connection with the body, so we cannot experience these vibrations yet.

THE WAVES OF THE ADHYAVASAY

All living beings have instincts like anger, ego and so on. Without instinct, worldly life cannot go on. And if there are instincts, they

— 31 —

need a place to reside. So they reside in the adhyavasay in the form of waves. The emotion itself is absent in the adhyavasay, but the waves are present in the form of instincts. When these waves move ahead, they become more concentrated. Thereafter, the waves are transformed into emotions in the field of leshya. Once solidified, the emotions are able to act at the physical level. We cannot experience the instincts when they are in the form of waves. But as they move forward, they become emotions and appear in the body as expression and action.

At the physical level, you see an effect of the emotional wave, but not the wave itself. For example, when someone gets angry, you do not comprehend the wave of the anger, but the manifestation of it. You see the effect, the symptoms in terms of words, gestures and physical moves and interpret that the person is angry. This is how you get to know the root emotion of the expression. The process of knowing the emotion goes by so fast you do not even notice it. In other words, we can say that this is a journey from the external to the internal world. Without the existence of the emotion inside, it cannot be expressed at the physical level. In fact, all the instincts, impulses and emotions exist within us; they appear at the physical level due to external conditions. If you know the true process of analysing the source of an emotion, you will start thinking beyond the physical to the subtle, passing through each field one by one – emotion, leshya, adhyavasay, kashay and finally pure consciousness. Doing so brings you from the physical level to the source of the emotion. It implies that the action you experienced on the physical plane is the manifestation or reflection of subtle consciousness.

Now the question arises, why does the consciousness send negative images to be reflected at the gross level? Is the soul or consciousness negative in itself? Of course not! Then how does conscious vibration become impure? There must be a reaction between the two. When the conscious vibrations pass through the kashay, which is the field of malevolent energy, they become contaminated. There is no way of preventing this. Whatever is reflected will always be impure. It means that there is no pure adhyavasay, no pure leshya and no pure emotions. Does it mean that we cannot have positive emotions and feelings like happiness, forgiveness and humbleness? We can. The positive feelings occur when the leshya is pure. But the leshya is pure if the adhyavasay is pure and the adhyavasay is pure if the intensity of kashay is less. The intensity of kashay depends upon the cessation of karma. Cessation is inversely proportional to attachment and aversion. In other words, purity increases if the feeling of like and dislike decreases. So there is a chain:

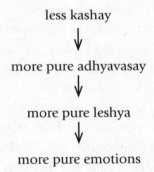

less kashay
↓
more pure adhyavasay
↓
more pure leshya
↓
more pure emotions

They are all interconnected and interdependent. Leshya can never be positive if the adhyavasay is not positive and adhyavasay will not be positive until the conscious vibrations coming out of the pure self bypass the field of kashay. Kashay has two time zones: low intensity and high intensity. Here 'to bypass the field of kashay' means that if the conscious vibrations pass through the kashay when it is at low intensity, kashay will not contaminate the pure conscious vibrations. If this happens, the conscious vibrations remain pure, positive and healthy. These positive vibrations construct pure adhyavasay which in turn creates positive emotions. This produces a healthy mind, healthy speech and healthy body.

~

So there are two factors behind purity and impurity – the less intense kashay leads to purity, while the more intense kashay leads to impurity. We can reduce the intensity of kashay through spiritual practice.

Practice can reduce the intensity of kashay. The more we practise the more we dilute the kashay. The purpose of spiritual practice is to calm down the kashay and to filter out the impurity of kashay from the pure consciousness. Thereafter, the resultant consciousness will be consciousness only in its pure form.

The preachings and teachings of the spiritual world are founded on this very idea of reducing kashay. Non-possessiveness, non-violence, truth, honesty, celibacy, forgiveness, contentment, compassion and charity – these are the ethico-spiritual principles propounded by Lord Mahavir to reduce kashay. For this, meditation, positive thinking and penance can help. We must also cut down possessiveness, violence, dishonesty, greed, and other negtive energies.

Cognitive knowledge is only the first step. The second step is applied knowledge, i.e., putting the knowledge into action.

DEVELOPING SELF-DISCIPLINE

Self-control or self-discipline is the first requisite to shrinking the kashay.

What is the beginning of the practice of self-control? Where do you start? The schools of psychology and spirituality, both ancient and modern, have discussed this and come up with certain similar and significant facts.

Leo Tolstoy believed that the first condition of meaningful self-discipline or self-control is fasting. The journey of self-control should begin with fasting. These are the thoughts of a man who was also known as an ascetic or saint of the modern world.

Lord Mahavir, who described twelve types of fasting, also said that self-control begins with controlling the diet. He said: '... begin self-discipline by fasting. For food is the greatest obstacle in self-discipline. Food creates laziness.' Tolstoy agrees: 'How can one overcome his laziness if he does not have control over his diet? And if he cannot beat laziness and non-vigilance, then how can he attain self-control? We have some basic instincts. If we cannot control those instincts then we cannot control other complex desires which are shaped by these instincts.' The desire to live, the desire to eat, the desire for sex and the desire for conflict are basic instincts. Every living organism has these instincts. If these are not controlled, other complex desires can never be overcome. Therefore the practitioner of spirituality must combat basic instincts, starting with the diet.

The first basic instinct is the desire for food, which is a significant instinct because our body gets activated by food. Food in its original form is of no use to the body. When we eat, the food is converted to energy. This energy drives our body and initiates a variety of actions. Our body has two important centres – the centre of bioelectricity (*taijas kendra*) and the centre of energy (*shakti kendra*). The centre of bioelectricity converts food into energy and the centre of energy stores it. The quality of energy depends on the quality and quantity of food. Remember that your mood and behaviour are driven by the energy you get from your food. So we can conclude that food is responsible for our moods and stimulates desires in us. Therefore, to control our desires we must control our diet. This is the first maxim of self-discipline.

The second maxim of self-discipline is regulating or disciplining your body. It is very necessary to regulate the actions and habits of the body. Until you develop new habits and your nerves are accustomed to new habits, a good personality cannot be developed. American psychologist William James, in his book *The Principle of Psychology*, says that good habits are necessary for a good life and good habits can be inculcated through practice. He mentions some tips for developing good habits which I would like to summarize:

1. To develop good habits, first of all think of the good habits, practise them and then restrict bad habits.
2. To develop good habits, train your body in a special way, because without training the body, good habits cannot take shape.

Our nerves and muscles are already conditioned to work in a particular way, and they maintain this trained condition unless they are reconditioned. For example, the body starts demanding sweets because the tongue is in the habit of tasting sweets. Your wish to act depends upon the pre-conditioned habit of your muscles. You do not pay attention to this habit consciously. Your muscles send a request to your brain. The brain accepts the request and the work is done. You are only conscious of the desire to eat sweets. So, when the habits of eating, thinking and acting are developed in the muscles, you eat, think and act in that particular mode.

Consciously, we don't even know how a habit develops. You perform an action once, twice, thrice. The more you repeat an action, the more your nerves fall into the habit.

Let's say you move into a new house and your bedroom is on the second floor. The stairs are a little slippery. The first time, you are very careful and go up and down the stairs cautiously. After a few days, when you are used to the slippery conditions, you pay less attention as you have made subtle adjustments over time. The muscles in your legs are trained, and the work is done.

Let's take another example. When you begin typing, you have to look at the keyboard to familiarize yourself with the layout of the keys. Over time, your fingers move to the correct characters without you needing to look at the keyboard. As the muscles and nerves are trained to move to the correct keys, typing becomes second nature.

Dr Williams tells us that when you want to develop a habit, do not make any excuse or exception, do not break the practice; continue on a regular schedule.

Suppose you begin meditating and your body starts getting used to it. If for some days you do not do it, then you start again, you will never perfect it. So, do not skip meditation for a single day. Be regular.

Lord Mahavir said that when you decide to do *pratikraman* (a process of self-analysis in Jainism), just do it. Don't skip a single day; do it regularly or it will not become a habit. To make your habit stable, keep practising till it becomes part and parcel of your life. Do not give break or pause until it becomes your nature.

There are other ways to regulate your body: yoga (*aasan*), breathing exercises (*pranayam*), relaxation, and so on. These exercises regulate your body, muscles and nerves in such a way that your body starts following your subconscious cues and you learn to control yourself.

The third maxim of self-control is *pratisanlinata* which means withdrawal of the sense organs from the external world and directing them to the internal world. This maxim tells you to hold back and to change the direction of your action. There are two types of action: natural action and action acquired through practice.

In nature, all things act in a mechanical process. Nevertheless, you can change some of the natural actions through practice. Your body has one specific place of inertia origination, which is the shakti kendra or centre of energy. It produces every desire and makes you eager to fulfil it. This energy centre is an attribute you are naturally endowed with. But you can change its mode of production by practising pratisanlinata. Therefore, to control yourself, you must go against your natural urges and learn to discipline the centre of energy.

Acharang, the first canonical text of Jainism, explores the fact that influx and outflow are the same, i.e., the path of incoming karma and outgoing karma is the same. The centre which is responsible for lust is also responsible for celibacy. The same knife that is used to kill a person can be used in surgery to save a life. The knife itself is not bad. Similarly, shakti kendra is not bad in itself. It depends on how you use the energy. It needs only transformation which comes through practice and by changing the utility of the energy flow. Through exercises and austerity you can convert the centre of lust into the centre of celibacy. This sadhana or austerity involves regulation of the sense organs. This is pratisanlinata.

You may wonder why there is a need to change the channel of your sense organs. *What is wrong with them? Are my senses not doing their job?* There is nothing wrong with the natural processes of your senses. Let us explore this.

The function of your eyes is to see. This is not bad. But when the object is relayed to the mind, the mind applies its own subjectivity, driven by emotions. Therefore, seeing is always biased by likes or dislikes. It is a natural phenomenon but it is not good. For, vision is not pure but biased by some force.

If you want to stay pure, you must control your sensory organs and remain indifferent to the object you perceive. There should be neither attachment nor hate for the object. You are neutral but happy.

Likewise, you need to control your kashay to develop purity and positivity.

Once, a very young boy came to see me with his father. The boy asked his father to write the boy's name in a book he was carrying. His father refused and told his son to use the book without his name written in it. The child was stubborn and began to pester his father. Finally, he started to kick his father. I was surprised to see so much anger in such a young child! Then I realized that anger is a natural phenomenon that does not need any training. So, there was no need to get alarmed.

Anger, pride and other negative emotions are all there at birth. But these can be changed through practice. Train the manifestation centre in such a way that it never shows anger. If you do achieve this, it will be a great achievement. The question is, how do we go about changing the centre? The answer is simple: one needs only to avoid the causes, situations and factors responsible for negative moods. Avoid the triggers and you avoid the anger.

Some people argue against this theory. They say, why should one stay away from the causes that are responsible for negative effects? Man should be bold enough to remain neutral; he should have the power to defeat and control negative emotions. He does not need to physically avoid the trigger.

Personally, I do not agree with this. I think such a theory is misleading. If you are not aware of the factors responsible for negative emotions, you can never get rid of kashay. The best way to reduce passion is to keep away from its stimulants.

Suppose a person has millions of dollars and many assets, and he does not use the money either for himself or for social welfare. Instead, he says, 'I am satisfied with my wealth. I am neither greedy nor attached to my assets. I keep them only for the sake of keeping them, no more. I do not care what happens to my wealth.' In my opinion, such people are only fooling themselves. Only one in a million people is selfless. Otherwise, there is hypocrisy everywhere. If in your worldly life you pursue wealth, how can you be detached internally? If you really want to minimize passions like greed, you will have to control yourself. The question is, how is this self-control brought about?

There are three components that are responsible for human activities – mind, body and speech. The functionality of all three is action. Action is by nature unstable and capricious; it is counter to all that is static and constant.

Take, for example, the action of writing or typing. Your fingers and hands have to move to perform the function. If they do not move, they cannot perform the activity. If you are planning to cook but close your eyes and relax, how will you do the cooking? Action needs movement. The mind, body and speech create changeability.

To control changeability you will have to change the channelling of energy and the direction of intent. This can be achieved through austerity, which gives us control over mind, body and speech. Regular practice of austerity (through meditation, breathing exercises, etc.) can change the habits which are with you from birth. Austerity is the process of minimizing the kashay.

Lord Mahavir has propounded three maxims for controlling the self and purifying leshya and adhyavasay: fasting, relaxation and disciplining the sensory organs. When you practise these, your kashay get reduced automatically. Remember, it is not that easy to achieve. There is a certain method to it.

First, you have to find out how the kashay gets nourished. What feeds it? If you hit and destroy the source that feeds the kashay, then it cannot survive. Let us search for the source together.

We have concluded that the mind, body and speech are all the source of nourishment. These powerful tools allow impurities to enter the body and nourish the kashay. When you begin fasting and regulating physical action and your sensory organs, negativity is reduced and eventually removed. When negativity is stopped, kashay starts losing power. When it is uprooted, consciousness emerges in its pure form. This is your ultimate goal.

In summary, we can say that there are two states – one is the state of pure leshya and pure adhyavasay, the other is the state of impure leshya and impure adhyavasay. The more you practise spirituality, the more you reduce kashay. And the more you reduce kashay, the more your adhyavasay, leshya, emotions, thoughts and actions acquire purity.

ESSENCE

A. *The gross and the subtle world*

❖ At first, you generally look at the action – for example, the symptom of anger.

❖ You do not focus on the emotion itself.

❖ When you go beyond the mind, you perceive leshya. We focus on the emotion but not on the energy coming from within.

❖ Moving forward, you perceive adhyavasay, this time only focusing on the energy. However, even here we do not reach the source.

❖ You move forward, reaching the ultra micro-body (karma body) and it is here that the source is actualized.

❖ The source or karmic body produces energy or waves. Later these waves turn into emotions and physical expression.

B. *How is it possible to control passion?*

❖ Through relinquishment or detachment.

❖ By developing good habits.

❖ Four steps to developing good habits:

   a. Analyse the effect of bad habits.

   b. Do not stop cultivating good habits until they are firmly rooted.

   c. Think in accordance with empowering the new habit.

   d. Internalize your habit and come alive through diligent practice.

C. *The foremost condition of a healthy life is self-discipline.*

❧ Fasting or control over food intake is the foremost condition of self-discipline

D. *Basic and complex desires grow in your body as a result of all this.*

4

The Connecting Cord of the Subtle and Gross Worlds

Every soul possesses two worlds – gross and subtle. Both are contaminated. Is there any bridge between these two? How can they be purified? How does one become spiritual? The answer is self-control together with self-purification. But this practice is obstructed, and the biggest obstacle is the ego. It is the ego that coaxes you to think of 'me first'.

Self-control is necessary for a good life. But psychologists don't agree with this assessment. Most psychologists assert that control or suppression does more harm than good. According to modern psychology, our emotions and feelings should not be suppressed because it results in malformed mental processes. If natural emotions are forcefully stopped, the suppressed emotions might create a kind of madness in the brain.

What modern psychology postulates is only partially true. It is true that using suppression and control as individual solutions within themselves can be harmful. But in the realm of the spiritual, suppression and rectification go hand in hand. Self-control is the path to self-purification. Self-purification is the end but self-control is the means, and without the means how can we achieve the end? Yet it is important to keep in mind the end goal – self-purification. The process of self-purification needs continuity. You should constantly put your efforts into purification in order to achieve it perfectly. Unfortunately, this does not always happen. The practice goes on for a little while and then comes to a halt. The continuity gets obstructed. And the biggest cause of this discontinuity is the ego.

The ego is like sweet poison – it works in such a manner that we rarely recognize its impact. Let's look at ourselves. None of us is perfect. We acquire bad impressions, bad habits and bad attitudes over the course of our life. If you are selfish, you will not help others if it is not reciprocated or if there is no immediate benefit. It is your ego that screams, 'Me first!' In some cases you do recognize that it is your ego at work, but even then, you are not able to modify your actions. Your ego does not let you introspect and change yourself. The ego says, 'I can never be at fault. What I do is always correct.' The ego is built by such feelings and it rules over the mind, preventing you from purifying the self. When you are dominated by the ego you neither feel nor show regret or acceptance for your faults nor do you appreciate the good deeds of others. In the end, an egoistic self cannot become spiritual.

At some point the ego gets dissolved in attachment or 'myness'. My body, my family, my house, my car, and so on. This 'my' is not different from the ego – it is an expression of the ego.

When the ego gets connected intimately with any object or person, it takes the shape of 'my'. So we can conclude that there are two manifestations of the ego – 'I' and 'my'. It is very hard to flush out the ego. Only a person who is disciplined can beat his ego. When you discipline yourself, you learn to keep yourself away from external stimulants and the forces of ego. Only then can you purify and discharge the ego.

The ego is very complex. It is hard to break it, but not impossible. The process of ego-purification involves two steps: spiritual study (*swadhyaya*) and meditation. Spiritual study means practice, effort and analysis of the inner self by studying the scriptures and through self-introspection. When this knowledge is concentrated and intense and you ponder deep into what you have learnt, it becomes meditation. Swadhyaya and meditation are similar in nature but they are two different states, like water and ice. Knowledge is like water, fluid and unstable, but when it gets concentrated it becomes as solid as ice. Thoughts are the best vehicle for the ego, so when thought is frozen, the ego does not have a medium for movement, and it is destroyed.

Once you know the technique of cutting the ego, you can move towards purifying the self. For this, you must learn self-control.

WHAT IS SELF-CONTROL?

Normally, self-control means controlling our food, sense organs, body, and so on. For a balanced worldly life, everything should be exercised in moderation. Self-control alone is not beneficial, and can even be harmful if not used correctly. Knowledge and meditation are the instruments of self-purification. If the tools of self-purification are not used with self-control, psychologists will be correct in their assertion that self-control brings about mental deterioration. Those who have realized their soul have pointed out that in order to have a spiritual life, to live an elevated or empowered life, both self-control and self-purification must be present.

> Once, Lord Mahavir was asked: Can knowledge lead to liberation?
>
> 'No, knowledge cannot lead to liberation,' Lord Mahavir replied.
>
> The next question was: Can faith lead to liberation?
>
> Lord Mahavir said, 'No.'
>
> The third question was: Can conduct lead to liberation?
>
> 'No,' the lord answered.
>
> The person who had asked the questions was very surprised that neither knowledge, faith nor conduct is the path to purification. He asked again: 'What is the path to liberation?'
>
> Finally, Lord Mahavir replied, 'These three attributes together lead to purification.'

THE CONNECTORS BETWEEN THE SUBTLE AND PHYSICAL BODY

We all have a dual personality. One is gross and the other is subtle. When we speak about the qualities in our physical body we are referring to our gross personality. When we are identified by the qualities of consciousness or soul then it is our subtle personality. You know you are a conscious being and that you are alive because the physical body has certain characteristics and functions that are found only in living beings and not in objects.

Your consciousness is what gives you life, physical activities and emotions. Your physical body is part of the material world. In general, a soul with the subtle body (karma body) alone is not accepted as a living being. People consider a soul with a physical or gross body, visible to all, as a living being. But the personality of a person depends on the subtle body. The subtle body has its own system, comprised of ten different features or factors, with which it projects itself at the level of the physical personality. These factors are:

1. *Gati* (birthplace)
2. *Indriya* (sense organs)
3. *Kashay* (passion)
4. *Leshya* (aura)
5. *Yog* (action/movement)
6. *Upyog* (conscious activity)
7. *Gyan* (knowledge)
8. *Darshan* (faith)
9. *Charitra* (conduct)
10. *Ved* (attraction for another)

These factors help the vibrations of the pure consciousness manifest themselves at the physical level. Actually, each of these factors contributes uniquely to building the personality. In spiritual science, it was quite difficult to explain the hidden facets of the human body in a scientific way. Fortunately, scientific research has made it possible to reveal and clarify these facets. For example, our body is composed of trillions of organic cells, without which our organs would not exist. Two thousand five hundred cells can be arranged in one inch. Each cell has 10,000 to 100,000 instruction codes. It is said that if you were to publish the instruction codes of a single cell, they would fill 2,000 volumes of the *Encyclopedia Britannica*.

As I have mentioned earlier, the micro-body has features that communicate with the physical body and give the body a living identity. The function of the features is to translate the subtle conscious codes into readable gross form, send them to the physical body and thereby give life and personality to the body. Without this, the body would not be recognized as a living organism. The body itself, without the spirit, is an inanimate object.

Let us discuss the ten factors responsible for our personality.

1. *Gati* (birthplace)

The first identifying quality of life is the gati, which decides your birthplace and life form. Gati creates four forms of life:

1. *manushya* (human)
2. *tiryanch* (animal)
3. *narak* (hellish soul)
4. *dev* (heavenly soul)

All human beings fall under the first category. Tiryanch includes the entire animal and bird kingdom, earth, water, fire, air and plants. Narak gati is comprised of creatures who go to hell after death. Dev gati includes all the deities and souls of heaven. These are the four forms in which a living being gets life after death. All four life forms can be further subcategorized into millions of variants. The effect of gati on the cell determines the life form that cell will take. Every living being has a unique cell pattern, which causes different effects on different cells. So the life form we take – animal, human, plant or any other – depends upon gati.

2. *Indriya* (sense organs)

Once the life form has been identified, the sense organs are determined. This station governs the functions of the sense organs. It is our sense organs that connect us to the external world.

3. *Kashay* (passion)

The third station is kashay or passion, which includes anger, ego, deceit and greed. Kashay is the third factor contributing uniqueness to living organisms and plays an important role in determining personality. This feature transforms the ultra micro-vibrations of passion into macro-vibrations and then transmits them to the physical body as emotions.

4. *Leshya* (aura)

The fourth station is the leshya or aura, which makes us sentient. Each unit of this universe, both living and non-living, radiates an energy known as aura. The aura is the energy field that surrounds the physical body. The aura of inanimate objects is static while the aura of a living organism constantly changes. It can be positive at one point and negative at another. Sometimes it has good colours, sometimes it doesn't. This is because of the changing field of the leshya within living organisms, which objects do not possess.

There are two types of leshya: *dravya* or physical leshya and *bhav* or psychical leshya. Essentially, leshya refers to the colour of conscious vibrations. Dravya leshya is in fact the atoms that constitute the leshya of a soul and bhav leshya is the state of consciousness that results from dravya leshya. For example, if one has padm leshya it means he has bright yellow atoms in his leshya. These atoms are dravya leshya and because of these yellow atoms he possesses positive and spiritual attributes. This state of consciousness is known as bhav leshya. So, we can say that bhav leshya is the effect of dravya leshya and the state where conscious vibrations are manifested at the physical level.

According to your emotions, your body radiates energy. These radiations surround the body and form an aura. Since the aura at the external level is the reflection of an internal conscious vibration, it keeps changing all the time. In comparison, the nature of an inanimate object remains the same at all times. So, while scientists can establish a universal fact about an object, they can never define the nature of a living organism. Today you are kind and passionate, tomorrow you may not be. I am not sure about your nature and, for the most part, neither are you.

You live in a house and the defining point of a house, it can be said, is to accommodate the occupant. For an inanimate object, there is no way to behave differently each time. The house will always allow to enter and live inside. It is you who has the choice to enter. Every living organism has choices. Even an ant has the choice to walk or stay in one place. This choice is because of freedom of thought or emotion. The faculty of emotion is so vast, strong and independent that it is beyond all laws and explanations. It cannot be confined.

In the difference between living aura and non-living aura, the bottom line is: objects do not have the capacity to change their aura. The aura of a living body is sometimes black, red, yellow, blue or white, varying according to emotions. When you get angry, your aura turns red. When you are cool and calm, your aura is white. So there is no doubt that a changing aura or leshya is a distinguishing characteristic of living organisms.

The field of leshya is where your emotions are shaped. The main function of the field of leshya is to convert conscious vibrations into the gross form and send them as hormones to the endocrine glands, brain and other parts of the body. The endocrine glands reflect the leshya.

Your emotions define your personality. In the field of leshya every signal becomes colourful in accordance with your past and present deeds and kashay. If the inner signal is influenced by anger, the field of kashay will give it the frequency of the colour red and the leshya will turn it red. So whatever goes in or comes out is colourful. The karma you attract always has some sort of colour.

The colours and cycle of emotion

There are two types of colours: bright and dark/dull. Someone who does any of the eighteen sinful acts like violence, anger, ego, greed, criticism, etc., as defined by Lord Mahavir, attracts black, dark blue, red, yellow or white. These colours make a person negative in thought and behaviour. On the contrary, someone who performs good acts attracts bright colours, which results in a positive personality.

Your journey to the field of leshya starts from the physical body. Then you will have to understand the colour of emotions to reach leshya. Each emotion is associated with some colour that is shown in the table below.

Emotions	Colour	Leshya
Impure emotions		
Uncontrolled desire	Black	Krishn
Unstable mind	Black	Krishn
Stressful mind	Black	Krishn
Craving	Blue	Neel
Crookedness	Grey	Kapot

Pure emotions

Controlled senses	Bright yellow	Padm
Peace of mind	Bright yellow	Padm
Control over food	Bright yellow	Padm
Stability of mind	Bright red	Tejo
Straightforwardness	Bright red	Tejo

Colour plays an important role in an individual's life. Recently, psychologists and scientists established that out of all environmental inputs, colour has the greatest influence on the conscious and subconscious mind, and on a person's emotions. Smell and touch also affect us, but the impact of colour is higher.

Colour influences not just our present life but also our next life. The colour we attract is responsible for our moods, emotions and behaviour. For instance, if at present you are thinking about hurting someone, you attract black. The colour you have attracted is encoded in the form of karma and sent inside your body, all the way to the conscious substance where it is stored. Eventually, this karma will rise and the same black atoms will pass through each field of your body and your emotions will be shaped accordingly. The quality of the emotions will be the same as the quality of the rising karma. If the rising karma is black, the emotions will be harmful. These emotions will be manifested at a physical, mental and verbal plane until you become a negative person. In this way you are negative in the past, present and in the future as well. It works as feedback mechanism. You get what you feed. It shows that the present is the result of the past and the foundation for the future.

In fact, consciousness is like a crystal. As we know, crystal does not have any colour of its own. It will, in a sense, take on the aura of the colour in its immediate proximity. Similarly, our soul or consciousness has no colour of its own; it takes on the colour that we attract to it. The colour you attract makes it colourful and defines the colour of your emotions and your mood. If you attract positive and bright colours, your emotions will be positive. It is a kind of cycle. We can convert a negative cycle into a positive one through conscious effort, righteousness, awareness and meditation. These spiritual activities result in the cessation of karma. After this, you attract bright colours, which will lead to a new, benevolent cycle and a new cycle of emotion too.

One who is born into life is subject to death. One who has died is reborn. Only the liberated soul never returns to this world. What you are born as in your next life – human, animal, heavenly soul or hellish being – depends on the leshya. The leshya during a person's death indicates the leshya of his next birth. For example, if your life is lost in the mist of negative emotions like cruelty and violence, you will go to hell. If during death you are compassionate, polite, calm and quiet you will be reborn as a human. Therefore, the outgoing waves of the present life at the time of death are the incoming waves of the next life.

There is no doubt that colour is connected with every aspect of life. It is manifested in knowledge or meditation, karma or life, death or rebirth. Even when we move our fingers, we radiate colour. Our face, heels, toes, knees, abdomen and every other organ have different colours. Obviously, the food we eat is colourful. Even when the food is processed inside the body, there is colour. Colour is associated with our thoughts, imagination and memory, which reflect our personality. Leshya, the identifying quality of colour, makes the greatest contribution to our personality.

5. *Yog* (action/movement)

The fifth identification of life is yog, which means action or movement. But how is yog unique to a living being? A table or chair can also move, even a tiny atom can be moved – but there is a difference between the two. Your actions – whether you speak, think, write, read, walk or sleep – are voluntary. You are not dependent upon others. Objects, on the other hand, depend on an external force to move them. Therefore voluntary action or yog is characteristic of living organisms. These actions can be physical, mental or vocal.

6-9. *Upyog* (conscious activity), *Gyan* (knowledge), *Darshan* (faith) and *Charitra* (conduct)

Other attributes of sentience – knowledge, faith, conduct, conscious activity and sexual desire – are also identifying characteristics of a living being. You know that this is a book but the book does not know that you are the reader. You have the capacity to know, to have faith, and to trust.

There is a very interesting fact about the conduct or behaviour of living beings as opposed to objects. Both have some kind of behaviour, but living organisms are variable in nature, while an object is fixed or constant in nature. For example, a person can be honest or dishonest, compassionate or cruel at different times. He has infinite choices but an object does not have any choice. A pen, for example, can only be a vehicle to facilitate the choice to write. It can't act like a car and a car can't act like a pen. Conscious activity is found only in living beings. Conscious activity, an activity guided by the consciousness, has multiple choices of action. Only a living being can perform certain actions that an inanimate object cannot.

10. *Ved* (attraction for another)

The last but not least identifying characteristic is the instinct of sex, the attraction for the same or the opposite gender, which compels a living organism to multiply and reproduce, which a non-living object cannot do.

In a nutshell, the aforementioned are the ten identifying qualities of a living being, stationed between the micro- (subtle) and macro- (gross) bodies. These stations modulate or translate the expression of the subtle to make it compatible with the gross level and contribute to the building of your personality.

ESSENCE

✤ There are two facets of personality – gross and subtle. Gross personality needs to be controlled; subtle personality needs to be purified. Only suppression or control cannot serve the purpose; purification is also necessary.

✤ Self-purification is the end while self-control is the means.

✤ The ego is the first obstacle in the process of self-purification.

✤ When you are dominated by your ego, you can neither feel nor show regret for misdeeds nor appreciate the good deeds of others.

✤ When you prevent negative energy from entering the body, the leshya becomes pure.

✤ There are ten stations between the gross and subtle body.

✤ The mediator between the gross and the subtle body is leshya, which transmits raw material from the gross world to the subtle world and supplies ready material from the inner world to the outer world.

5

Transforming Your Personality – I

If you change your leshya, you will change your personality permanently. When the leshya is changed, thinking is changed; and when thinking is changed, behaviour is changed. There is a whole chain from leshya to behaviour.

Every mature person wants to update and renovate himself. Typically, almost everyone has the mindset for personal and progressive behaviour modification. But the question is: how do you transform your personality and where should you start?

These are significant questions. But these queries arise only when you want to change yourself. If you have the desire to change, you should. The next step is deciding what kind of change you want. You can change yourself in basically two ways: 1) hide your weaknesses or 2) delete your weaknesses.

For example, your office is untidy and you want to clean it. You can do so in two ways: You can collect all your belongings and put them in a closet. Or you could put all your belongings in their proper place and discard what you don't need. In the same way, you can clean your personality either by hiding your weaknesses or by organizing your qualities and purging your shortcomings.

Let's explore this idea further. Most people are inclined to hide their shortcomings. They do not want to present themselves as they are. They mask their true inner self by projecting an artificial persona. This is why it is very hard to recognize the core personality of a person. And a person does not wear just one mask; he has multiple faces which hide his real self.

For example, a man can be both angry and hypocritical. Knowing this, he goes to extraordinary lengths to hide these negative qualities and project himself as cool, calm, kind, simple and transparent. In such a situation, how do you recognize a person's true nature? The most mysterious entity of the universe is the human being. It is hard to understand human nature. An object cannot deceive anyone, but a person can do so, because of posessessing a rational mind.

Transformation is quite different from hiding one's personality. Transformation results from a structural inner conversion. It gives rise to a new personality. But this transformation can be both positive and negative. It means that a good person can transform into an awful person and a bad person can change into a good person. The constant endeavour to transform the personality can make a person pure.

As a matter of fact, in this world, you will never meet someone who is totally evil or angelic. A good man will have some malevolent qualities and an evil man will have some good in him. Good and evil go hand in hand. The only difference is that of margin and focus. If good qualities predominate, bad qualities stay in the margins. If the bad qualities are in focus, the good ones are not as apparent. We possess both but only one is on the surface at any given time. It is important for us to understand which part of our body produces negativity so we can transform our personality. Research shows that the leshya is the psychic centre that can bring about this transformation.

Let us remind ourselves of the three levels of the body – gross or physical body, micro or taijas body, ultra-micro or karmic body – and the three levels of consciousness associated with them – gross consciousness, leshya and adhyavasay consecutively. Chitta, mind and the sense organs are related to the physical body. Leshya has nothing to do with the physical body. It generates emotions and is the most active conscious centre of the body. While your thoughts, speech and actions depend on your physical body and muscles, leshya doesn't need muscles to perform.

WHAT MAKES UP OUR PERSONALITY?

There are three features of personality – emotion, thought and behaviour. Behaviour is physical while thought is mental, but both are connected with muscles. Emotion is not a muscular exercise. Emotions do not operate from the muscular-skeletal realm, they are an output of leshya. Behaviour can be controlled quite easily. Even your thoughts can be controlled, by focusing on your breathing and with some other exercises. But when you enter the world of emotions, control has less impact. It is impossible to give up all inner impurity. You can be determined not to eat sugary foods or resolve that you will go for a walk every day, but it is impossible to decide that you will never get angry or project an ego or any other passion. We cannot control our emotions permanently, but we can certainly purify them.

We often decide to change ourselves but nothing works. Our resolution, commitment and determination get left behind. You might decide not to get stressed about things. But when you find yourself in heavy traffic, you can't help getting stressed. You are firm in your resolution initially but as the situation lingers, your resolve wears thin. So now what? How can you stay with your resolution for ever?

You can. Change your perspective, change your process.

When you make a resolution, it is your mind that is at work, and mental activity is a muscular activity that cannot help you get rid of emotions. You can control yourself but you cannot eliminate emotions. It is only by gaining access to the field of leshya that you can change the emotions before they are transmitted to the physical body. You need to awaken your consciousness through meditation in order to change your personality. Once your personality is changed, there is no need for control on a physical level. If you reach the state of *shukla leshya* (white aura), *padm leshya* (yellow aura) or *taijas leshya* (red aura), you have transformed your personality. You will be detached from all material things. In this state you do not need any external control.

Earlier, I discussed emotion, thought and action. Thoughts are more tangible than emotions and actions are external and hence the most visible of our expressions. You can hide your emotions but you cannot hide your actions. Some people are very cruel but behave properly in public. There is no bridge between the internal and external personalities. They are at two extreme ends. The external personality can cheat you, but the internal personality, the field of emotion, can never cheat itself. Therefore, the criterion to know your personality is neither the mental world nor the behavioural world, but the world of emotion.

In ancient times, a spiritual leader would examine the ability of his disciples through the disciple's aura. Your aura reveals your emotions and your personality. Modern technology has developed tools like cameras and the polygraph to scientifically 'see' the aura and emotions. When a person is connected to it, this equipment can tell if he is telling the truth or whether he has committed a crime. What this equipment actually reads is mental activity. But the human mind is clever. When the criminal understands what the machine is doing, he simply changes his flow of thought. The apparatus reads his thinking pattern and the reading is now incorrect. So, these tools can give you an erroneous reading. But an aura can never cheat you because it is the mirror image of your true emotions.

Modern science has discovered that any disease appears in your aura three months before it manifests itself in your body. So, if we can find out about the onset of a disease earlier, we can begin preventive treatment sooner.

The lives of heavenly souls (deities) also have a certain time-frame. Six months prior to their death, their aura starts diminishing; this is the truest indication of their decease in the present life and their transition into the next life.

The aura carries the signals of our subtle world from this life to the next. It is the aura that brings all psychic expression and karmic vibrations to the emotional level.

⁓

You are familiar with language and script. When you think of something, your mind conjures a mental image. There is no language there. When you think, there is a picture; when you speak, it becomes script. A person who has extra-sensory perception can read your mind by capturing the mental picture of your thoughts. You may wonder how this process manifests. Is it possible to know the mind of another person even if they do not speak? Yes it is.

When you think, images are snapped on your mental screen. By the time you finish the thought, these images come out in the form of energy and are dispersed throughout the cosmos. The pictures do not last for ever in your mind but are ever present in the cosmos. Later, even thousands of years later, a person with the ability to read minds (*manah-paryav gyan*) can recognize these images in the cosmos and can read the thoughts of those who were here thousands of years ago.

There are infinite mental images in the cosmos. We speak in terms of certain sounds or words that are part of the physical plane. In other words, we can say that the language of our mind is the image and not the word. But emotions are prior to thought. So the language of emotions is more subtle than that of the mind, which is in the form of a line. Adhyavasay is more subtle than emotion. It is in the form of vibrations. So when we move from the gross to the subtle world, our language also becomes subtle.

- The language of adhyavasay is through waves or vibrations.
- The language of leshya is in terms of a straight line.
- The language of the mind is through images.
- The language of the body is through sounds or words.

Our physical activities are the expressions of inner vibrations. Psychologists explain this differently. According to psychology, behaviour is an effect of situation. For example, a person sometimes feels love and at other times is filled with hate. You could dislike someone in the morning and feel affectionate towards the same

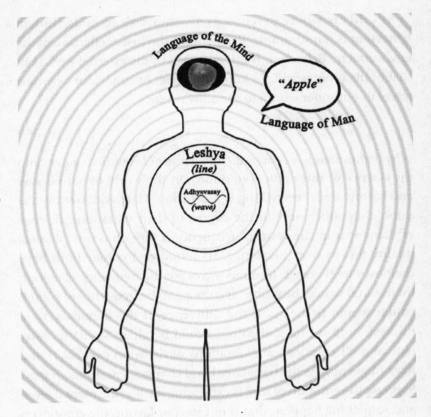

LANGUAGE OF ADHYAVASAY, LESHYA, MIND AND BODY

person in the evening. Why does human behaviour change so frequently and so drastically? Behavioural psychology says that a man behaves according to his surrounding objects and environment. Humans start learning from childhood. When a mother loves her child, the child learns to love. Sometimes the mother scolds the child, and from this the child learns to express anger. We learn and frame our behaviour based on the behaviour of others.

But this is where psychology reaches a dead end. Human behaviour is not so simple. Behaviour is not just a reflection of the environment. Behaviour is not an image of the external world but that of the inner world. To know the secret of behaviour, we must travel to our inner world, to the adhyavasay.

~

Why do humans have contradictory natures? Let us first understand the essence of this nature (emotion). In the world of adhyavasay and karmic body, everything is a delusion. Hate and love are the same, they differ only in the degree of their vibrations. Science explains this in the form of frequency. Every object or physical quality has its own frequency. So sound and colour both have their own frequencies. If sound waves got the frequency of colour, then sound would be visible. If colour got the frequency of sound, colour would be heard. If the difference in the frequency were bridged, both sound and colour would be alike. Similarly, love, hate and all emotions are vibrations of delusion (*murchha*) and have frequency. As the frequency band changes, emotions change. Suppose the emotion of love is expressing itself at the mental level, and something happens that is not in your favour, the emotion is changed and gets the frequency of hate. There may be other causes for the change of frequency. As I mentioned earlier, there is an incessant flow of conscious vibrations from inside, influenced by our rising karma, which builds our emotions. The nature of the conscious vibrations also gets changed because of change in the nature of karma. Therefore, if the effect of karma is of love and the next rising karma is that of hate, the conscious vibrations that were carrying the emotion of love will now be affected by hate and will project the same at the external level. Consequently, the picture on your mental screen will also change. Your thoughts will be full of hate. In the same way, anger, ego, deceit, fear, greed and lust are all deluded vibrations with different frequencies.

Your emotions are different states of one wave. Eventually, they get manifested in your life. So, a child doesn't learn to love and hate only from his mother, but the flow of love and hate also comes from within. Emotions exist inside us but manifest at the physical level when external forces trigger them. The root of our emotions lies within us, and is the source of our personality. Therefore, if we understand the mechanisms of the subtle and gross worlds, we can transform our personality.

⁓

If you want to change your personality, this change is possible at the conscious level of leshya. If leshya is good, the personality is good. If leshya is evil, your personality will also be evil. If you change your leshya, you change your personality. By changing the leshya, even a criminal can become a calm sage while a sage can turn into a criminal. It is not merely an external change but an internal one. When leshya is changed, thinking is changed; when thinking is changed, behaviour is changed.

There is a whole technique of change. Behaviour can be changed only through discipline or control. Thoughts can be changed through discipline. Positive and negative thoughts exist simultaneously within us but are effective one at a time. When we are positive, there are no negative thoughts and vice versa.

If you want to change your behaviour, you need to change it entirely. Partial treatment will not work.

Consider the difference between ancient and modern methods of medicine. If your knee is injured, the cure provided by medical science will focus only on the area of pain and not on identifying its source. In ancient times, the doctor would treat the whole body.

They went in deep and got to the source of the pain. This approach ensured that the pain disappeared. So ancient methods treated the whole body, uprooted the underlying problem and cured the disease, while modern methods focus on the indicator organ, which controls the disease but doesn't cure it. Furthermore, modern medical methods have potentially harmful side effects.

Like ancient medical techniques, self-purification can be achieved by going to the root of the emotions. But self-control, on the other hands, is like modern medical science, which can control behaviour only for a while.

A person who wants to upgrade the positive attributes of his personality will have to control his inner shortcomings. The first step to this is self-control. He will have to control his mind and sense organs. The degree of control increases with the person's social hierarchy. For example, a person who is the head of a company or organization needs to control ego and anger. The control should be reflected in his behaviour, as behaviour reflects personality. Spirituality has an unseen presence, but our behaviour shows outwardly. Society does not take note of your inner purity. It evaluates your external behaviour.

The mind and the senses along with speech and behaviour patterns all need some sort of control. But if your leshya is black and you are attracting black energy incessantly, you will have negative thoughts. You might decide a thousand times not to use inappropriate language; you might listen to the preaching of your spiritual leader hundreds of times. But as different situations arise, you lose your control and you find yourself doing and saying things you later regret. This is the effect of krishn leshya. Krishn leshya does not let you stay in a good emotional space. With krishn leshya, black atoms drive your emotions. These emotions drive your thoughts, words and actions, and you end up saying and doing something you will probably regret.

THE LIMITATIONS OF OUR EFFORTS

We think we can change our habits and we make the effort to change our behaviour by controlling ourselves. The effort to change the habit works up to the conscious mind, gross body and muscular system, but it changes our habit only for a short time. We often try hard to control an unwanted act, but we are unable to stop. What can be the reason?

Rakesh is an aggressive man who wants to control his anger. He applies some remedies like drinking water, changing locations, rhythmic counting and keeping quiet for stretches of time. These tips help him control his anger temporarily. But whenever the unexpected situation occurs, he gets upset. All his efforts fail. Why does this happen?

Lord Mahavir has said, 'O soul! You are my friend and foe as well.'

How can a soul become both friend and foe? This is because the benevolent state of the soul becomes your friend and a malevolent state of the soul becomes your foe. Everything has its limitations. If you do not connect the outer world with the inner subtle world, if you do not connect the thoughts, behaviour and gross consciousness to the leshya and adhyavasay, you can never solve the problem. Therefore, to transform your personality, you need to focus on the inner subtle world.

Why did Rakesh fail to correct himself? It is because of his leshya and because there was no connection between his leshya and his effort. He was not trying at the level of leshya and emotions.

The effort he made was external so its effect would go only up to the muscular level. He continued to attract negative energy from the cosmos and create a bad aura.

So, without understanding the internal world, your external effort is of no value. External control alone can never cure the problem. To cure the problem, you must change the colour of your aura.

The ascetic and the householder both want to develop control over the sense organs, mind and emotions. But how do we do that? Can mere self-control solve the problem? It is hard. So what should one do? We must go beyond the boundary of control and think about the effects of colours. If you really want to transform your personality, then change the colours you are attracting through your thoughts. If you attract bright yellow (padm leshya), you can develop self-control. Each colour has its own attribute. Bright yellow colours help us develop intellect, bliss, happiness, wisdom, positive attitude, enthusiasm and inner abilities. You are inclined to go to the inner world because of it. But if you attract dull black (krishn leshya) or blue (neel leshya) you will always behave badly.

In conclusion, to change your behaviour and change your aura, change your leshya first. Then your efforts will not be in vain.

ESSENCE

✤ Man wants to change.

✤ There are three constituents to one's personality:

    1) Emotions (which need to be purified)

    2) Thoughts (which need to be controlled)

    3) Behaviour (which needs to be disciplined)

✤ To purify the emotions, awaken the field of leshya. The field of leshya is the generator of emotions and is the most active and alert conscious centre.

✤ The field of leshya gets influenced by the internal and external atmospheres.

✤ When you gain control over negativity, the external influences become ineffective. Then the field of leshya or emotions gets empowered and it neutralizes all the negative signals coming from inside. Once the inner negative signals are neutralized, they do not come into effect at the physical level.

✤ Both malevolent and benevolent emotions have specific colours.

6

Transforming Your Personality – II

The endocrine system is the origin of your nature at the physical level,
but the source of your nature lies elsewhere. Your instincts, emotions and
habits arise in the field of leshya. If you want to change your habits then
change and purify your leshya.

Self-purification and self-control are inter-dependent. Self-purification only occurs once self-control is achieved, and without self-purification, self-control is incomplete.

Self-purification is not mere sublimation. It is the complete transmutation of your personality. Once this happens, there is no way you can go back to your old habits. Sublimation, in psychology, is a process of channelling impulses or energies; it is a process of changing the direction of habit. Sublimation diverts the flow of instinctual energy from its immediate aim. This process does not change the nature from its root, it only changes the direction. The instincts remain. For example, if a person has the instinct of sexual desire, when it is sublimated it might be manifested as art.

Self-purification is not about sublimation. It is about destroying your old nature and building a new one.

Let us first discuss the source of our nature. There are two significant systems in our body: the nervous system and the endocrine system. At the physical level, our nature and habits originate in the endocrine system. Once our habits are born they manifest themselves as a physical characteristic of our behaviour. In the endocrine system, our habits are stored in chemical form. These chemicals travel to the brain, from where the nervous system becomes stimulated to manifest our nature to the world. Science describes this as the neuro-endocrine system.

Remember that the endocrine system is responsible for your nature at the physical level, but your nature is grounded in your leshya. The first step to changing your habits is to purify your leshya. Before we understand the process of purification, let us first look at the way in which leshya is responsible for our bad habits.

There are six categories of leshya:

1. Krishn (black)
2. Neel (blue)
3. Kapot (grey)
4. Tejo (red)
5. Padm (yellow)
6. Shukla (white)

Increment of prosperity

Krishn $\rightarrow$ Neel $\rightarrow$ Kapot $\rightarrow$ Tejo $\rightarrow$ Padm $\rightarrow$ Shukla

Black $\rightarrow$ Blue $\rightarrow$ Grey $\rightarrow$ Red $\rightarrow$ Yellow $\rightarrow$ White

Of these, the first three are negative in nature while the other three are positive. Krishn, neel and kapot are responsible for bad habits and immoral acts such as cruelty, violence, crookedness, dishonesty, greed, cheating, sensual desires, laziness, etc. Our physical body has the corresponding centres of leshya where attitudes are generated. Adrenal glands and gonads are the agents of these three leshya. The emotions of these three (black, blue and grey) leshya are produced in chemical form inside these glands.

According to modern science, gonads are the place where sexual desire is produced and negative emotions like fear and aggression are stimulated. In Patanjali yoga, the places of these two glands (adrenal and gonads) are called *swadhisthan chakra* and *manipur chakra*.

In yoga philosophy there is a book called *Atma Vivek* that explains that cruelty, enmity, attachment, disobedience and mistrust are stimulated in the swadhisthan chakra while greed, jealousy, fear, attachment, passion and sorrow are stimulated in the manipur chakra. The third chakra, anahat chakra, is located in the heart. Craving, violent deeds, expectations, worry, ego, etc., are stimulated here. According to yogic philosophy, these three chakras – swadhisthan, manipur and anahat – are responsible for our instincts.

The science of leshya says that all negative habits are generated in these three leshya.

Leshya	Negative Attitude
Krishn	lack of self-discipline, anger, cruelty, lack of compassion and lack of sensual control
Neel	jealousy, ignorance, deceit, sensual desires, aggression and craving for food

Kapot   crookedness, hiding one's flaws, possessiveness, false spiritual beliefs, revealing other's secrets and speaking badly of them

Now compare the three schools of thought: physiology, yoga and leshya. Adrenal and gonad glands in physiology, swadhisthan, manipur and anahat chakras in yoga, and krishn, neel, and kapot leshya – they are almost analogous.

The science of leshya says all negative habits are generated in these three leshya. Yoga philosophy says these habits are the products of three chakras. And physiology explains that bad habits or emotions are produced in the gonads and adrenal glands.

~

THE MOVEMENT OF ENERGY WITHIN THE BODY

Negative attitudes in the body travel from the abdomen to the navel and then to the heart. Once you understand this, it becomes easy to facilitate change.

We can divide our body into three parts:

1. Upper body: the area from above the navel to the top of the head
2. Middle body: the area around the navel
3. Lower body: the area below the navel

Evil attitudes arise in the middle or lower body and in a small section of the upper body too. When your mind is at the middle or lower part of the body, the psyche and vital energy move down and activate lower areas like the adrenal glands and gonads, which produce evil thoughts and make you materialistic and negative. Conversely, if you are materialistic, energy will flow to the lower body and activate the lower glands. If your energy travels repeatedly from the lower body up to the shakti kendra, the root of the spinal cord, evil attitudes become a habit. For example, thoughts about sex or envy are initially not very intense But if you keep thinking about it, it becomes a habit. By the time you realize this, it is too late. Now the question is: how can you reduce negative instincts? Is there a way? Of course there is, but first you have to train your mind to stay in the upper body, above the heart, so that you keep the energy flowing upwards. Never let it travel low. When your mind is in the upper part of the body, the energy moves upward and activates the positive centres in the body. If your mind remains in the upper body, your habits will start to change on their own.

Lord Mahavir says that the incoming and outgoing doors of energy are the same. In other words, what comes inside goes outside and what goes outside comes inside. It is a continuous cycle.

Acharya Jeetmalji, the fourth spiritual leader of the Terapanth sect of Jainism, supported the fact that there is a whole cycle of behaviour. Our present behaviour is the effect of our past karma. He said that the karma that comes into effect in the present was attracted in the past and our present attitude binds new karma. When it matures, the accumulated karma comes into effect and forces us to behave according to its nature. Suppose, in the past, you committed a violent act which attracted bad karma. When the karma of violence is ready to give results, it reaches the leshya, and is then converted to hormones in the endocrine glands. Thereafter, these hormones reach the brain, which instructs the mind and muscles to act violently. As soon as you behave violently, new bad karma is attracted and attached to the soul. In due time, they will give the same result. This is how the cycle repeats itself.

The energy attracted due to negative deeds has many colours.

Gautam, the chief disciple of Lord Mahavir, asked, 'O Lord! How many colours, taste, smell and touch are found in activities like violence, lying, stealing?'

Lord Mahavir replied, 'These actions are endowed with two colours, two smells, five types of taste and four types of touch. Anger, ego, deceit and greed also possess these qualities. The energy of these habits is unconscious. Therefore, these attitudes are endowed with colour, taste, smell and touch. This colourful energy develops new habits when it enters our glands.

Is there a way out of this whirlpool? Yes, there is. Otherwise there would be an everlasting chain of karma and nobody could come out of it. Preksha meditation, which helps you focus deep within yourself, can help you come out of this cycle of karma by changing the direction of your mind. But there is another problem with the mind: it thinks in two ways, either with attachment or with hate. In other words, the mind reacts in two languages: I like or I dislike. Both emotions are negative.

When you engage your mind in preksha, it forgets negativity and goes directly to the consciousness. During preksha you go beyond feelings; you are with your pure self. There is no evil and therefore no karmic bondage. All that exists is the radiation of pure consciousness.

Gautam asked Lord Mahavir, 'What are the colours, taste, smell and touch associated with abstinence from violence, lying, stealing, non-celibacy, anger, ego, deceit and greed?'

Lord Mahavir replied, 'These states are free of colour, taste, smell and touch. For, these are the states of consciousness.'

In conclusion, to stay with negative emotion is to stay with the physical world and to stay away from negativity is to stay with our consciousness. The former is colourful while the latter is colourless.

In preksha meditation, we observe the sensations or vibrations in the body without being driven by emotion and likes or dislikes. Whatever we experience at the physical or mental level has corresponding sensations and vibrations inside the body. These vibrations are a function of our nervous system. Every organ or chemical has some sort of vibration. For example, if you feel pain, there will be certain vibrations inside the body. Similarly, warmth, cold, pleasure or anger have corresponding vibrations. But our unstable mind does not allow us to experience these vibrations. When we meditate, we can experience the vibrations of the organs. During meditation we merely observe the vibrations without any reaction. If there are heat vibrations, we do not think it is too hot and dislike it. When the vibrations are of pleasure, we do not respond positively to them. We remain neutral. This state of chitta is known as *sharir preksha* or 'perception of body' in preksha meditation, where we perceive the micro movement inside the body. When we experience these vibrations we start realizing the subtle vibrations of chitta and at a deeper level the vibrations of the consciousness. Therefore, sharir preksha makes the body instrumental to understanding and experiencing the consciousness.

CLAIRVOYANCE

Sthanang Sutra, the second Jain canonical text, explains an interesting theory about clairvoyance. Clairvoyance is a knowledge attained by the purity of the consciousness. It means that you know what is happening around the world without using the sense organs or any external instrument. You have information from three periods of time: past, present and future. The depth of knowledge depends upon the degree of purity. The person with clairvoyance gains knowledge directly through his consciousness. The consciousness does not need the sense organs to comprehend something.

Because of our karma, our soul is unable to know anything without the help of our body. Therefore, when we see, our eyes help our consciousness to perceive the depth, shape and colour of the visual spectrum; when we hear, our ears help our consciousness know the sound of the aural spectrum. Our consciousness is not directly connected to the world, so the body becomes a medium. And when clairvoyance is attained our consciousness becomes pure, our body and mind also become pure. So there is a direct connection of the consciousness with the world.

PRACTISING PREKSHA MEDITATION

There are three steps in preksha meditation to develop purity:

1. Apay vichay: thinking of your weaknesses and obstacles
2. Vipak vichay: thinking of the outcome of the present problem
3. Sansthan vichay: analysis of the shape and the constituents of the universe

The clairvoyant understands this process of analysis and uses it to achieve knowledge. He knows the external world through his body, either through his whole body or through a particular part of his body. For instance, if the right shoulder becomes *karan*, then he focuses there and knows the world through it. The general definition of karan is purity.

In this context the word 'karan' stands for purity of chitta and shapes on the body because of the purity of the body. The chitta drives our body, mind and speech. It is the representative of consciousness at the physical level.

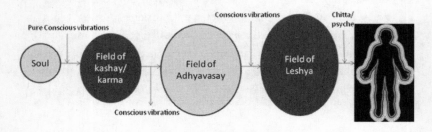

FLOW OF CONSCIOUS ENERGY FROM SOUL TO BODY

The purification of chitta is the main purpose of preksha meditation. When the chitta is purified, you will be able to know the world directly and your attitude also becomes positive and pure.

Purification means 'awakening of consciousness'. As we know, chitta pervades everywhere in the body, but it is not pure everywhere. When I say that chitta gets purified, it either means that the entire chitta is purified or that the chitta in a particular area of the body is purified.

If the entire chitta is purified then any part of the body is clairvoyant. But if the chitta is only partially purified then only that purified part of the body is clairvoyant. So if the chitta of a person's right shoulder is purified, the chitta does not need the help of the brain or any physical organ to know the external world. The chitta gets a direct connection to the world and knows the world.

It is interesting that the body gets purified along with the chitta. When any part of the body becomes pure, an auspicious figure or shape is transpired on that part of the body.

In Jain yoga, there is a good description of the shape found on the body. Auspicious shapes represent purity, while inauspicious shapes denote impurity. According to Jain Acharya, there are many more auspicious shapes formed in the body in addition to kamal and chakras. These are Swastik[1], Nandyavart[2], Kalash[3] etc. There are thirteen psychic centres (chaitanya kendra) in the body where consciousness is intense. Until the higher awareness is awakened, all psychic centres have inauspicious shapes like that of the chameleon. When these centres are awakened by meditation, our inner consciousness gets purified and the inauspicious shape or pattern gets changed and becomes auspicious.

---

[1] Swastik: signifies peace and well-being
[2] Nandyavart: indicates nine types of material, mental, physical and spiritual wealth and treasure
[3] Kalash: signifies wisdom and fullness

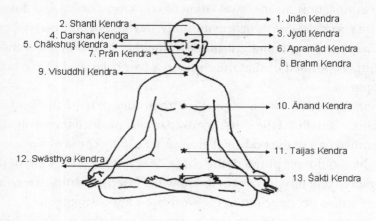

2. Shanti Kendra
4. Darshan Kendra
5. Chākshuṣ Kendra
7. Prän Kendra
9. Visuddhi Kendra

1. Jnän Kendra
3. Jyoti Kendra
6. Apramäd Kendra
8. Brahm Kendra
10. Änand Kendra
11. Taijas Kendra
13. Śakti Kendra

12. Swästhya Kendra

PSYCHIC CENTRES IN THE BODY

When the shape of your upper psychic centres changes by awakening, the navel itself begins to get purified.

When psychic centres are awakened, it facilitates changes in your process of thinking. To purify your thoughts it is necessary to stop your mind from travelling downward. Your mind and chitta should not go beyond the navel and abdominal region; rather it should move upward to the heart, throat, tip of the nose, eyebrows and head. When meditating you should focus your mind on the upper body so that the psychic centres in the upper body get awakened. This upward trip of your mind and conscious energy brings about a change in the glands due to which the hormones are changed, and finally habits are changed.

Eventually, krishn (black), neel (blue) and kapot (grey) all change. It happens step by step. First, krishn is converted to neel, then neel to kapot. Kapot leshya when purified becomes tejo (red). The whole scenario of thinking and habit gets changed once the colour of leshya is changed. As we discussed earlier, leshya is a kind of conscious wave and vibration. So tejo leshya is the first milestone in the path to spirituality. Each wave has its own colour. Every colour has its own effect. Krishn leshya is black, which is negative in effect, whereas tejo leshya is the colour of the rising sun. The colour of tejo leshya belongs to the red family, which is good for spirituality. When the tejo leshya increases, the energy in your body starts changing too.

Each wave has its own characteristic and effect. During krishn leshya, the waves have a high frequency and a short wave length. In neel leshya, the frequency is reduced while the wave length increases. In kapot leshya, the frequency reduces further and the wave length increases. In tejo leshya and padm leshya, the frequency decreases while the wave length increases. As the wave turns into shukla leshya, the frequency is reduced to zero and the wave becomes a straight line; only the wave length remains. This is the state of a complete, integrated and stable personality.

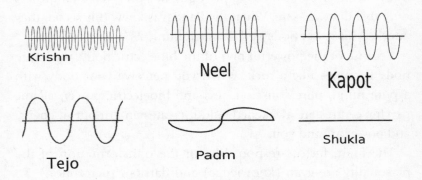

FREQUENCY AND WAVE LENGTH OF LESHYA

Once your body is purified your knowledge and intuition are revealed. The chain of attachment is broken and inner strength is awakened. The power of perception increases. Your bioelectric power gets strengthened. In this state you become powerful and if you look at any person, your eyes emit a powerful energy, so strong that the person you are looking at also becomes so powerful that nobody can harm him. We often feel that if we are in the presence of a pure soul, negative energy cannot have an impact on us. This is possible only through meditation.

This is what had been seen in Indian mythology. In the *Mahabharata*, when Gandhari, Dhritrastra's wife, looked at her son, Duryodhan, his body became as strong and stiff as a rock. When the war between the Kauravas and Pandavas began, nobody was able to attack him, not even great warriors like Bhim and Arjuna. They could not understand the secret. Finally, Lord Krishna told them to attack the lower body which was not as strong. When Gandhari projected her sight on Duryodhan's body, only his upper body became like a rock because he was wearing clothes on his lower body, below the waist. His upper body was uncovered and it was only this that was safe. When the Pandavas knew this secret, they attacked his lower body and defeated him.

Because of the powerful rays of the bioelectric body, the entire body becomes like a rock. When you perceive your body with a pure mind, pure consciousness and bioelectric power, all the psychic centres are awakened, and it creates an armour of energy and power around you.

The main factors responsible for the transformation of the personality are gyan (knowledge) and darshan (perception). To know and to perceive are the greatest tools of transformation. Without yarn, there can be no cloth, even if you have the best machines. Similarly, without these two powers – knowledge and perception – you cannot attain purity. You do not need to bring these powers from outside. They are already there within you, but they are dormant. Meditation helps you awaken them. These powers help your mind know and purify the endocrine glands. Purified endocrine glands purify the field of leshya, because endocrine glands send energy to leshya. Once the hormones of the glands are pure, the leshya becomes pure. Leshya purifies the adhyavasay, which later reduces the intensity of corrupt indulgences, thus eliminating an evil habit.

There is thus a chain involved in the re-construction of personality. Each station of this chain affects the other.

ESSENCE

Tools to transform the personality:

- Contemplation – mantra chanting
- Colour meditation
- Analysis of disadvantages of negative emotions
- Perception of body is flawed
- Perception of psychic centres

❖ Negative attitudes arise in the middle or lower body and a small section of the upper body too. When you think of the middle or lower part of the body, the energy moves down and it activates lower areas like the adrenal glands and gonads, which produce evil thoughts.

❖ Personality transformation is possible through the purification of leshya. The purification of leshya is achieved with purification of the endocrine glands. Endocrine glands can be purified through preksha meditation.

❖ To know and to perceive are the greatest tools of transformation.

❖ The person with clairvoyance gains knowledge directly through consciousness. The consciousness does not need the sense organs to comprehend something.

7

A Process of Transmutation
of Your Instinct

*Everyone wishes to attain peace of mind, have a stress-free life, love, peaceful
co-existence, generosity and so on. Spirituality is capable of providing such a
haven. When the journey of tejo leshya begins, the vibrations of spirituality
are awakened. When the vibrations of spirituality are awakened, your
transformation begins. If you want to achieve spirituality, you should start with
kayotsarg (relaxation). When you are relaxed, the intensity of desire slows down.
When you gain control over your sensual desires, your spiritual journey starts.*

Man wants to take shelter in the sanctum of spirituality to
acquire inner peace and happiness. Spirituality is the best
personal refuge, one that protects us from every evil. We wish to be
spiritual in order to acquire the qualities we feel are lacking as well
as to discard the evil that is part of our nature. A non-spiritual life
allows space for wicked habits and thoughts along with fear, hatred,
worry, stress, jealousy and so on. No one likes to go through life
bearing the burden of these vices. The aim always is to stay away
from them. Ultimately, every individual strives for the positivity
that comes with a peaceful and happy life.

It is good to seek the sanctity of spirituality and to follow practices that bring spiritual awareness. However, self-doubt will occur when you feel you have not attained any positive personal growth as a result of your practice. This indicates that there is a problem with your methods, commitment, or some other aspect of your practice. It also shows that you are not practising with proper diligence or that the path you are moving on is not a spiritual one. Do a self-assessment to determine where the problem lies. This self-analysis can lead to a real change in you.

If you have mastered your spiritual self, your spirituality will be projected in your behaviour. In a spiritual person, tejo, padm and shukla leshya begin to manifest themselves acutely. By observing the character of a person, you can accurately assume the level of spirituality of that person. You might ask: what are the essential characteristics of one who has a spiritual presence? The answer is described in the following couplet:

Audaayam daakshinyam paap-jugupsaa cha nirmalo bodhah,
Lingaani dharm-siddhe praayen jan-priyatvam cha.

One who is benevolent, accepts everything most favourably, stays away from sin and has pure, crystallized knowledge that makes his words true and is dear to all, is spiritual.

These are the core defining characteristics of a spiritual person.

A spiritual person never thinks evil, speaks evil or acts evil, because all his activities and knowledge are motivated by pure consciousness.

How does one develop the qualities of spirituality? This can be achieved by changing your leshya and aura. If you transform your aura from krishn, neel and kapot to tejo, padm and shukla, you can change yourself. Without changing the leshya you cannot change yourself. The transformation is not the subject of knowledge or expression, but it is the subject of experience, the subject of practice.

Karl Marx said very correctly that philosophy gives only knowledge; it does not change one's life. Today, religion has become like philosophy. A person is engaged in endless rituals, but at the end of it, does not find any change in his life and behaviour. Consequently, the result of religious activity is negligible. We start with nothing and end where we started, reaching nowhere. If there is no change in life after practising rituals, it is obvious that religion only develops an attraction to rituals. Is this the true image of religion?

In such a situation we are forced to recognize that while we love our religion and its rituals, we must ask ourselves if it changes our lives. The fact is that spirituality is hidden under religious activity. The ritual is not spiritual in itself but it is the outer surface of spirituality. If you have not been changed through your efforts, then it is not the fault of religion, it is the faulty illusion that ritual brings a spiritual life to those who pursue it. And if you are truly spiritual, you will definitely change.

Spirituality begins with transformation. While you are in krishn, neel and kapot leshya, you will be cruel, greedy, arrogant. As you practise spirituality, your leshya begins to change into tejo. When the journey of tejo leshya begins, the vibrations of spirituality are awakened and transformation starts to take place. This indicates that you are becoming increasingly positive, cool, polite and soft. With this change, you begin to feel the positive spiritual vibrations. You have in all likelihood never experienced such inner happiness and tranquility in your life. As you enter the domain of spirituality, the whole scenario changes and your thinking pattern also gets transformed. Now you start realizing that the pursuit of material things cannot give you everlasting happiness.

In preksha meditation, when you concentrate and meditate on the *darshan kendra* (centre of intuition), which is located between your eyebrows, your leshya is converted to tejo and you start to feel its bright sparkling vibrations, and a unique experience of inner bliss. The aim of finding happiness in the material world eventually diminishes and disappears. Your thoughts are transformed as your nature and habits also change. This is how spirituality works. In my opinion, if spirituality does not change your negative thoughts, habits and behaviour, the practice is worthless. Meditation should be incorporated into religious activities.

The greatest process of personality transformation is meditation. You can thoroughly change your personality through regular practice of preksha meditation. You simply have to set a goal and visualize the image of the goal and think: 'I am purifying my consciousness and mind; I have to discard all evil habits that are produced by the inner impurities.' After setting this goal, start meditation with the perception of your body. Undertake a mental trip over your entire body starting from the toes up to the head and observe the vibrations or sensations wherever they happen in your body. After that, shift your consciousness to your breath and practise taking long and deep breaths. After this, focus on the psychic centre to awaken the consciousness. This practice of meditation brings a positive shift in your personality. You do not consciously notice the transformation. It happens in a very subtle way. As I said earlier, it is not the subject of knowledge but the subject of realization.

Many practitioners of preksha meditations have changed themselves. The practitioners themselves did not know the reason for such a transformation.

Russian scientists once attempted to solve an ubiquitous societal problem – tobacco addition. Acupuncture was used on the subject to attempt to cure his addiction. This experiment was carried out for five days. There are three parts of the ear – inner ear, middle ear and outer ear. Each part has certain acupoints. Scientist pricked the skin in the middle ear. The results were amazing. Fifty out of the seventy patients who were smokers were completely relieved of their addiction and the remaining twenty reduced the frequency of their smoking.

In fact, if an addicted person meditates on his ear, which is a centre of vigilance (*apramad kendra*), he can get rid of any addiction. This is because a particular area of your ear has the power to stop your addiction. Through preksha meditation one can awaken the power to control and stop the urges of an addiction. Many chain-smokers and alcoholics have given up their addictions by practising preksha meditation.

Preksha meditation involves three major elements: perception (*preksha*), autosuggestion (*bhavana*) and contemplation (*anupreksha*). Preksha meditation is not just for perception or observation; it is also a technique for transmutation. Autosuggestion is also a tool to modify old habits. This gives validity to the idea that autosuggestion is a perfect way of transformation.

Lord Mahavir said, 'The one who purifies his consciousness through bhavana is like a boat in water.' It means that such a person can swim away from the ocean of birth and death. Through bhavana you can rectify your bad habits. Thereby, you achieve the purity of consciousness and come out of the cycle of birth and death. For a person who practises bhavana, it is not difficult to overcome the evils that affect daily life.

Indian philosophy and literature describe the practice of bhavana at length. In Vedic literature it is written that ancient Indian sages developed and maintained power through positive autosuggestion. For instance, they would say: 'May my vocal power always be active. Let vital energy flow incessantly in my nerves. Let my eyes have good sight. May my ears be endowed with strong hearing capabilities.' These positive autosuggestions helped them live a long life.

Just as positive thinking is a force of long life, negative thinking and an inferiority complex are causative forces in reducing your life span. When negative energies permeate your thoughts, they erode your entire physical system, ultimately leading to death. This is why bhavana is so important. Bhavana or autosuggestion is an active force. On the other hand, being negative is another, more destructive way of autosuggestion. Thus there are two types of bhavana, positive and negative, and both have their own effect.

In this context I would like to refer Dr Emile Coue, a physician who formulated the Laws of Suggestion. In his book, *Self Mastery through Conscious Autosuggestion*, he writes:

> I know certain people who predict in advance that he will have a sick headache on a certain day, in certain circumstances, and on that day, in the given circumstances, sure enough, they feel it. They brought their illness on themselves, just as others cure theirs by conscious autosuggestion. But if our unconscious is the source of many of our ills, it can also bring about the cure of our physical and mental ailments. It can not only repair the ill it has done, but cure real illnesses, so strong is its action upon our organism.

In his opinion, autosuggestion is an instrument that we possess at birth, and with which we play unconsciously all our life, just as a baby plays with its rattle. It is, however, a dangerous instrument; it can wound and even kill you if you handle it imprudently and unconsciously. On the other hand, it can save your life if you know how to use it properly. One can say of it, as Aesop said of the tongue: 'It is at the same time the best and the worst thing in the world'.

Autosuggestion is useful in treating moral complaints and physical ailments. In the same book, Dr Coue describes an experiment he performed on an eighteen-year-old boy, who had conceived a violent hatred against his brother and felt impelled to stab him. Dr Coue treated him using suggestion, and the result was marvelous. His hatred for his brother disappeared, and they got along very well after that. The doctor followed up on the case for a long time, and found that the cure was permanent.

Once, a professor did several experiments in order to study the impact of autosuggestion. In one experiment, he began with an instruction to his subject: 'I am giving you a very hot spoon. When you pick up the spoon, it will create a strong burning sensation, causing you to burn yourself. Now please pick up this spoon.' As soon as the subject picked up the spoon, he experienced a burning sensation. He got blisters on his hand. The spoon was cold, but he still got burnt. Why is this? It was the effect of autosuggestion. Everybody has an inner field of consciousness, leshya or bhavana. When any thought transcends to this level or up to the level of bioelectric energy, this field sends the signal back to your physical level and to the cosmos to manifest the thought. The field of leshya affects the bio-chemicals and, consequently, the brain sends corresponding signals to the muscles. In this instance, the object did not affect the person's consciousness but conscious thinking affected the entire scenario. In this manner, any thought you bring up to the inner level becomes true. It is not magic but a fact.

In another experiment, doctors chose a perfectly healthy subject and told him that he was suffering from a fever. Over a short period of time, he was made to consult several doctors and was given the same diagnosis each time. Over this time, the suggested fever became a reality, eventually reaching 104 degrees Celsius. After a while, another doctor gave him a new diagnosis: 'Who told you that you have a fever? You are absolutely healthy.' After a couple of hours, his temperature returned to normal. His fever manifested and went into remission without any physical cause.

⁓

Sometimes people get angry without any reason. Why does this happen? The Jain canonical text *Sthanang Sutra* explains a few causes of anger. One of these is self-produced anger, when you get angry without any external reason. You might be angry thinking of something that happened in the past or by anticipating the future. In the same way, ego, fear and hate can also be stimulated without external cause.

We are very familiar with the emotion of fear. When you are alone you might become obsessed with thoughts of someone attacking and robbing you. After that, whenever you are alone, whether it is day or night, you become so afraid you feel like you are being tortured. This fear comes from within; it is your own negative energy that makes you ill. The external environment alone is not responsible for your ill health.

The founder of homeopathy, Dr Samuel Hahnemann, said that germs are not rooted in the disease but that the root of a disease is a deeper affliction. In fact, the disease is rooted in leshya. When the leshya is pure, you remain healthy. Whenever the leshya becomes impure or malevolent, you fall ill. You do not realize this right away. You realize it later when it is manifested at the physical level.

When you change the leshya with autosuggestion you are self-healing your body. When you give positive suggestions to yourself and those suggestions reach your leshya, your energy changes and positive energy enters your body. This is how bhavana helps to cure illnesses.

MANTRAS AND HYPNOSIS

Along with autosuggestion, self-hypnosis and mantra chanting are also instrumental in bringing about change.

A mantra is a special combination of letters. When chanting mantras you keep repeating the same words over and over. Through this repetition, positive sound waves and vibrations are generated and go into the inner depths of your spiritual self. Your vital energy finally reaches the leshya. After a length of time, which varies with the individual, the great wave of the mantra stills all other vibrations. The vital energy produced by the mantra changes the quality of the leshya. This is the moment when the transformation is initialized. This connection of your inner bioelectric energy with vital energy is the awakening state of the mantra. It is only at this stage that the mantra becomes effective and the personality is changed.

These days hypnotism is also used to change habits and attitudes. Hypnosis is a mental state. It is usually induced by a procedure known as hypnotic induction, which is commonly composed of a long series of preliminary instructions and suggestions. Hypnotic suggestions may be delivered by a hypnotist to the subject, or may be self-administered (through autosuggestion).

TECHNIQUES OF TRANSMUTATION: HOW TO PRACTISE BHAVANA

We know that bhavana works in transforming the personality, but the internalization of knowledge is not enough to bring change. We need to learn the correct methodology of practising bhavana.

We must know the ways that will help us carry our external or gross energy to our inner conscious level.

1. *Kayotsarg*: Total relaxation of the body
2. *Anupreksha*: Self-analysis or contemplation. This involves two steps:
    *   *Apay vichay*: Reflecting on the disadvantage of the attitude
    *   *Vipak vichay*: Analysis of the outcome of the attitude
3. *Vivek*: Discrimination between dos and don'ts, true and false
4. *Dhyan*: To meditate on the centre of intuition (located between the eyebrows)
5. *Sharan*: To take refuge in or to recognize the infinite knowledge, intuition, bliss and power residing within
6. *Bhavana*: Repetitive autosuggestion to develop positive attitude
7. *Vyutsarg*: Auto-therapy (giving up old habits)
8. *Pratipaksh bhavna*: Instil a new positive attitude (such as forgiveness in place of anger)

KAYOTSARG

The first step is *kayotsarg* (relaxation). For practising bhavana you have to completely relax while being fully aware. Kayotsarg stops your muscular movement. Staying still ensures that your energy is directed and expended inward as opposed to the outward direction of energy that occurs when muscles are active. Therefore, to create a smooth flow of energy, kayotsarg is necessary. According to the Jain scriptures, kayotsarg is an integral part of life. When a Jain monk returns after going out, on returning, he first relaxes before proceeding with any other task. This balances the nervous system and muscular system. He also practises kayotsarg right before he studies, meditates and sleeps, after waking up and before and after *pratikaman* (self-introspection). He is also compelled to relax after performing an undesirable act (if unintentionally done), as a sign of regret for the misdeed. In these cases, kayotsarg is done as a perception of breathing by focusing the rhythm of breathing. The recommended number of breaths varies from one activity to another. It may be eight, twenty, fifty, hundred or thousand.

In kayotsarg, we relax the entire body from the head to the toes and release all the toxins and stress from our body.

Each organ of your body is important. In acupuncture therapy it has been proved that all conscious and psychic centres in your brain are also located in your hand. The energy points of the entire body can be found in your hand. You can control your body by controlling your hand. So, by relaxing your hand, you can relax your brain too.

Your feet and toes also contain psychic centres and gland connections. Your big toe has connections to the pituitary gland, eyes, ears and more.

Our ancestors said that we can improve eyesight by massaging the big toe with oil. This might sound surprising but it is true. You can cure your eyes and ears through your toes. You can control the secretion of the pineal and pituitary glands through your big toe. Your toes have connections with the whole body. You just need to stimulate them.

Acharya Bhadrabahu, a great scholar and Jain spiritual leader, practised mahaprana dhyan for twelve years. Someone who gets into mahaprana dhyan is completely disconnected from worldly affairs. He is in a state of such deep meditation that it becomes difficult to bring him back to his normal state. There is only one way to bring him back – press the big toe.

Jain Acharya Pusyamitra was practising mahaprana dhyan. One of his disciples, Uttar, was taking care of him. Uttar was the only disciple who was aware that the guru was in mahaprana dhyan. After a few days, when the other disciples could not find their guru, they began to doubt Uttar. They accused Uttar of killing the guru. The news reached the king of the land. He came and enquired about Acharya Pusyamitra. Uttar replied that Acharya Pusyamitra was meditating. The king gave orders that he wanted to meet the acharya at once. Uttar went inside and pressed the big toe of his guru and the acharya terminated his meditation.

What is the relation between meditation and the big toe? Deep meditation happens when you focus deeply on the *jyoti kendra* (centre of enlightenment) and *darshan kendra* (centre of intuition), located at the big toe. This is the intersection point of the gross and subtle bodies. Once you have access to this intersection point you are in the state of deep meditation (*samadhi*) and mahaprana dhyan.

The third most important part to relax is the vocal cords, which are responsible for creating thoughts. So when you relax your vocal cords, your thoughts are affected too.

When you get control over your hands, legs and vocal cords the rest of your sense organs relax by themselves. And when you are relaxed, the intensity of your desires slows down. When you are in control of your sensual desires, your spiritual journey begins.

HOW TO PRACTICE KAYOTSARG

The first step of kayotsarg is to recite a resolution. The resolution states that kayotsarg is a way to get rid of all miseries and to change your habits. It is very hard for someone who does not know the process of kayotsarg to change his personality and habits. Whether you want to change your habits or cure a physical ailment, you have to do kayotsarg first. Relaxation is also the first step of the self-hypnotism technique.

To recite the resolution stand straight, fold your hands and close your eyes. The resolution is:

> I practise relaxation to change, to correct, to atone, to cleanse unwanted habits; to purify the mind, to cure the wounds of evil, to clean negative energy, to destroy the atoms of karma and to eliminate the delusion created as a result of bad habits, which have enveloped the body and mind.

Freeze all physical activities, and relax your muscles. The foremost condition to achieve peace is inactivity. If you want to achieve spirituality, you should start doing kayotsarg.

1. Choose a comfortable posture – standing, sitting or lying down. When lying down, keep your feet apart and hands a little away from your body. Keep your eyes softly closed. Still your body and slow down your breathing.
2. Take your mind to the big toe of your right leg. Relax all muscles and cells of the toe. Stay there for few a seconds then shift your mind to your other toes, foot, heel, calf muscles, knee, thigh, buttocks and up to your hip-joint, relaxing each of them to experience the lightness. Do the same on your left leg.

3. Now make a mental trip from waist to shoulder, front and back. Relax your lower and upper abdomen, chest cavity – heart, lungs, ribs, collar bone and shoulders. Stay for a few seconds on each organ.

4. Relax your back from lower back to shoulders.

5. Relax both hands from fingers to shoulder. Be aware and experience the relaxation.

6. Loosen up your neck muscles, vocal cords, entire face from chin to forehead.

7. Allow your head and brain to relax.

8. Experience that your whole body is relaxed. There is no pain or stress.

9. Take three long breaths and conclude the kayotsarg.

ANUPREKSHA

The second step is *anupreksha* or self-analysis. In this process you need to analyse the habit you want to change. It can be hate, greed, jealousy, ego, negative thinking and the like. For this you have to practise self-introspection. It includes two steps.

1. *Apay vichay*: Reflecting on the disadvantage of the attitude.
2. *Vipak vichay*: Analysis of the outcome of the attitude.

You are supposed to ask some questions to yourself about the harmful facets of your bad habit. Self-analysis is also the second step of hypnotism. If you want to get rid of your anger you have to first ask yourself: Why is anger bad? Why do I want to get rid of it? Is anger really harmful?

Once you start analysing, you get into deep self-examination and you learn about the disadvantages of anger. You find out that anger is turmoil. When it appears at the physical level, it weakens you. It is a disorder of the brain, heart and the adrenal glands. When you get angry, the brain is targeted first and it goes out of control. The brain's neurons get excited and need more energy to work. As the brain demands more energy, the other organs of the body are deprived of energy, you start feeling restless, and your whole body gets affected. It does not end here. The next target of anger is the heart. When you are angry, your heartbeat increases and it behaves abnormally. The third target is the adrenal gland. When you are angry, the adrenal gland secretes higher quantities of adrenaline. This extra effort makes the adrenal gland weak. In this way, anger drains the strength out of the brain, heart and adrenal glands, the most significant organs of the body.

By analysing it repeatedly, you see the outcome of anger and you realize that you should combat it. Next, you ask whether you can combat the anger. After analysing, you find that you can. You find the positive solution: *I have infinite power within. Therefore, I can combat my anger.* This realization of capacity is the last step of anupreksha.

Similarly you can work to overcome greed. You can introspect on the benefit of having more desires and greed. Is it really making your life peaceful, happy and healthy? Is it helping you enjoy life? Then you realize that you are enslaved by your high ambitions and desires, which give you stress rather than long-term happiness. You are running after your desires, not enjoying the life you have. Greed leads to competition, envy, revenge and so on. It ruins your life. Moreover, you are earning money to stay happy, but also using it to regain your health and happiness. Therefore, it's better to limit your desires. You must follow your need not your greed. Your constant awareness can definitely develop the satisfaction and the ability to live with rational desires.

This very analysis is the foundation for transformation.

VIVEK

The third step of transformation is *vivek* or insight. This is the stage of reasoning or discrimination. Here, you reason with yourself: I can give up anger or any negative emotion because it is not my nature. If it were my nature, I would never be able to get rid of it. I am full of knowledge and bliss but anger hides my knowledge and bliss and destroys my strength.

Through critical reasoning you distinguish yourself from anger and conclude that anger is not in your nature.

When you accept that anger is not a natural phenomenon and you are not destined to be angry, the problem is close to the solution. You do not have any doubt. Once everything is clear, you are ready to practise. As Lord Mahavir said, *'Padhamam nanam tao daya'*, which means 'Knowledge is the precursor of action'. Knowledge is power. When you have the knowledge, it is easy to follow.

DHYAN

The fourth step of transmutation is *dhyan* (meditation). Focus your consciousness at the darshan kendra (centre of intuition). This is the centre of extra-sensory knowledge and inner vision. When you meditate towards the darshan kendra, your autosuggestions affect you very quickly. Without any thought you try to feel the vibrations taking place over there. The more you are focused the deeper you get. Psychology tells us that the suggestions that reach only your gross mind never work. They cannot bring about a change in your personality. You need to ensure that your autosuggestion reaches a deeper level of consciousness. It must reach your leshya and adhyavasay.

SHARAN

The fifth step of transmutation is *sharan* (to get shelter), a concept that is unique to meditation and not found in hypnotism. You might wonder where one goes to get shelter. You can get the shelter of yourself, the shelter of your own power, or you can get the shelter of your deity, owner of infinite knowledge, intuition, bliss and power. The shelter of these four infinities is very significant. It awakens the taijas shakti. You develop the confidence that your inner power will definitely help you change your attitude. This confidence will not let you give up the practice. During this period the electric waves are so intense you start feeling the transformation right away.

There was a Sufi saint, Khaiyad, who was very spiritual. One day, he was passing through a forest. At prayer time, he lay down his blanket and started to pray. His disciple did the same. As soon as they began their prayers, a lion started to roar. The disciple got scared. He took his blanket and climbed up a tree, but the saint continued sitting quietly. The lion came, walked around the saint, and went away without causing any harm. When the saint finished his prayer, the disciple climbed down from the tree and they continued their journey. They had hardly walked a mile when suddenly a wild dog came before them. As soon as the saint saw the dog, he tried to defend himself with a stick.

The disciple was surprised to see this reaction. He exclaimed, 'Gurudev! What is this? When a lion came, you sat quietly, but now when a dog is before you, you are ready to fight with him. I do not understand.'

The saint explained, 'While I was in prayer, my god was protecting me. I was in the shelter of god. But now you are with me, not my god.'

If you get the shelter of your god, if you get the shelter of the four infinities, then your bioelectric body gets connected to your consciousness. Your bioelectric waves are so powerful that you will not be scared of anything. As you take the shelter of the four infinities, the waves of infinite knowledge, intuition, bliss and power start moving around you. You feel like you are filled with infinite knowledge, intuition, bliss and power. This is the moment when your transformation starts taking place. Eventually, this transformation gets concentrated and becomes permanent, and you are changed.

BHAVANA

The sixth step of transmutation is bhavana. Let's understand the process. When you sit to meditate, disconnect yourself from the external world and focus within,. Then mentally tell yourself:

I want to get rid of anger. I am getting rid of it. I do not want to be angry any more. The waves of anger cannot stay around me. Anger cannot stimulate me. Anger cannot affect my brain and muscular system.

Keep saying this to yourself firmly. Make yourself aware. Your suggestion should be strong enough to reach your inner consciousness. When you repeat the same thought, your chitta gets empowered by the same energy.

Any object, when given the same environment of sustained energy for long periods of time, gets empowered and coloured by that environment.

When water is poured into colourful glass bottles and kept in the sunlight, it gets empowered by the sun's rays and by the colour of the bottle. The power of plain water and of water that has been empowered by the sun are quite different. Water empowered by the sun's rays becomes medicated, and can cure even incurable diseases. Likewise, milk, sugar, vegetables and other food can also be empowered. If you put water bottles on a magnet, the water gets magnetized. This magnetized water has healing powers. When food or liquid is kept in the sun, its quality changes. Similarly, one who is a master in mantra-chanting can empower water by a mantra. Such water can solve any problem, physical or mental.

You can take one positive thought and empower yourself by repeating that thought for five to ten minutes. This process creates a mental environment to help you accept the new habit. Try to take your thoughts to your subconscious mind. Repeat the positive thought for a long period of time. In the beginning, repeat the sentences in a loud voice. Gradually, reduce the volume and finally repeat the suggestion mentally. Colour your mind with the thought, then take your suggestion to the deepest level of your consciousness. You are now ready to adopt the new habit.

VYUTSARG

When your mind and consciousness have been empowered with the feeling of adopting the new thoughts or habits you want to develop, only then do you move forward to the next step, *vyutsarg* or relinquishment. Now repeat the sentence: 'I am relinquishing my old habit and nature. Now I do not have any connection with my old habits.'

Until you disconnect the relation of 'I' and 'mine', the old habit cannot be changed. You will have to leave 'I' and 'my'. You will have to say: 'Now I am giving up this habit. I am disconnecting my relation with it. This habit is not mine now.' When you firmly disconnect the connection, then promptly say: 'I will never repeat this habit again. I will be alert and aware of it in the future.'

PRATIPAKSH BHAVANA

The last step of transformation is to instill the anti-emotion through self-suggestion. There is one more step after removing old habits – developing new ones. Even after eradicating anger, there is room for it to come back. So you need to fill the space with positive reinforcement.

The opposite of anger is forgiveness. Shut the doors of negativity and replace your anger with forgiveness through auto-suggestion: 'The attitude of forgiveness is developing. I will forgive myself and others.'

Similarly we can replace other negative emotions too. We can counter ego with humility, crookedness with straightforwardness, and greed with contentment.

This is the complete process of transformation of one's nature and habits. Generally, people say that human nature can never be changed. But that is not true. If this process is followed regularly and diligently for two to three months, you will certainly succeed in changing your nature. The time it takes might vary from individual to individual as there may be differences in faith, will power, inner strength, inner purity and so on. But irrespective of these differences, there will be no difference in the result.

Without a strong belief in transformation, the process of self realization is not possible. A *mithya drishti* (one who lacks faith) cannot become a *samyak drishti* (a person possessing strong faith); a samyak drishti can never become a *vrati* (a person who takes small vows); a vrati will never become a *mahavrati* (a monk who practises the five great vows of non-violence, truth, non-stealing, celibacy and non-possessiveness); a mahavrati cannot become an *apramatta* (one who is completely aware of his own self); an apramatta will not become a *veetaragi* (one who conquers attachment and hatred); and a veetaragi will not become a *kevali* (omniscient).

THE SPIRITUAL TEACHER

Spiritual science is capable of developing spirituality; a teacher is capable of transforming his students.

In Andhra Pradesh, a spiritual teacher was teaching his five hundred disciples. He focused his thoughts on making them intelligent as an experiment of positive thinking. Amazingly, all of them became intelligent, brilliant and wise.

I would like to share a personal experience. I was very weak academically and in my early childhood I was usually at the bottom of my class. But once I received the guidance and blessings of my guru, Acharya Tulsi, my transformation started. I became sharp in almost everything – the field of knowledge, intelligence, nature and behaviour.

~

If you follow the process of transformation, you will become successful in changing yourself. It will take you from the bottom to the top. If you don't, you will remain where you are. The question is: Why do some people not change? There are two reasons for this: either they do not know the process or they do not follow the process.

I would like to re-emphasize that if a religious person does not change, he is not religious in the true sense. The religious leader who does not introduce any programme to change his followers is not a real leader and is not aware of his duty. When the followers want to change and the spiritual teacher gives them a plan and a process, the spiritual experience becomes glorious. Spirituality is transcendental; it gives you what the material world cannot.

Today, crime is rampant in society. In spite of increasing materialistic comforts, crime has increased. Lack of wealth and excess of wealth are both harmful and both motivate crime. This proves that material comfort cannot solve the problem of evil and crime. It cannot change habits. We need spirituality. Only spirituality can reduce crime and remove evil habits.

In preksha meditation, right after relaxation, the practitioner makes a resolution that he is practising meditation to purify his mind and to remove the habits caused by an impure mind. If you start meditating with this resolution, your whole energy drives you to change your habits and purify your mind. Start your meditation with this resolution each time, and you will face the day ahead with a new personality and good habits.

ESSENCE

❖ Your behaviour is the outer projection of your inner spirituality.

❖ A spiritual person never thinks evil, speaks evil or acts evil, because all activities are motivated by pure knowledge.

❖ As your leshya becomes tejo and you begin to feel its bright and sparkling vibrations, the experience of inner bliss is unique.

❖ Just as positive thinking leads to a long life, negative thinking and an inferiority complex are causative forces in reducing your life span.

❖ Bhavana or autosuggestion is the best way to uproot inner demons. Old habits are moved out and replaced by new, more constructive ones.

❖ Take one positive thought and empower yourself by repeating that thought for five to ten minutes.

❖ Once your mind and consciousness are empowered with the habit you want to develop, drop the old habit.

❖ Until you disconnect the relation of 'I' and 'mine', the old habit cannot be changed.

8

Transforming Your Attitude through Colour Meditation

If you stay in krishn, neel or kapot leshya, you gain the world but lose your soul. Try to make your inner persona prosperous. Your inner self is the foundation of your outer manifestation. Inner and outer peace together make for a complete social life. Otherwise, your life will be barren.

There are three tools for strengthening our inner self:
1. Preksha meditation
2. Bhavana or autosuggestion
3. Colour meditation

In earlier chapters we looked at preksha meditation and bhavana. In this chapter we will learn about colour meditation.

Once, the dark colours went to Goddess Lakshmi and said, 'Without money we do not get honour and respect. So we ask that you be with us all the time wherever we are.'

Lakshmi responded, 'All right, I will do so. But tell me one thing, what type of person is your greatest attraction?'

The colours replied, 'We like a person who is narrow-minded, selfish, irrational, greedy, negative, aggressive, arrogant, lazy, evil, stubborn and cruel. We also like someone who does not have self-control, hates everybody, does not respect anyone, is not receptive, speaks harshly and is dishonest and jealous – this is our attraction.'

Lakshmi faced a dilemma. She had already promised to go with the dark colours, but after hearing about the kind of people they liked she knew it would be difficult. She could not renege on her promise but she accepted the proposal on one condition. She said, 'Okay, I will stay with your beloved ones, but not internally. Instead, I will stay as their external wealth, which can give those people external comfort but not mental peace.'

The colours agreed and Lakshmi went with them.

Later, the bright colours went to Lakshmi with the same request.

Lakshmi asked them the same question: 'Who are your favourite types of people? What are the qualities of your family members?'

The colours replied, 'People who are polite, simple, stable, transparent, content, spiritual, cool, calm, peaceful, positive, compassionate and balanced, who speak less and are the well-wishers of all.'

Lakshmi replied with a pleasant smile, 'I like such people too. Do not worry. I will stay in their heart in the form of peace.'

There are two things that are constantly pursued by man – comfort and peace. While wealth can bring you material comfort, there is no guarantee that it will bring peace. On the other hand, you can be at peace but have no wealth. Comfort is a consequence of external wealth while peace is considered internal wealth.

People who have tejo, padm and shukla leshya have inner wealth, the wealth of peace. They might suffer physically or financially, but these circumstances do not stress them.

This shows that it is bright colours that keep you peaceful and not dark colours. The soul that has krishn, neel and kapot leshya can get material comfort but it lacks mental peace and inner happiness. On the other hand, someone who has tejo, padm or shukla leshya will always be peaceful and balanced. No adverse situation will disturb your peace if you have spiritual wealth within.

The great sage Milarepa was close to death and suffering a lot of pain.

His disciples asked him, 'Gurudev! Are you in pain?'

He replied, 'Not at all. I know that there is pain everywhere in the world. But I do not feel pain, for my mind is at peace.'

Those who have peace of mind never feel pain. To have pain and to experience pain are two different states. There is pain in the world. The mere existence of pain does not fill you with pain, but when you experience it you feel the pain. And it is up to you to experience it.

While doing preksha meditation, if you merely observe the pain and its sensations, you won't experience it. And sometimes, when you distract yourself with other work, you forget your pain.

Once, a man experienced a pain in his heart. The doctor came to see him and he described his pain to the doctor.

Suddenly, the doctor said, 'Sir, I am feeling very ill. Please help me.'

The patient became nervous. He gave the doctor some water.

The doctor drank the water and slowly seemed to get better. The doctor told him, 'Sir, my payment please.'

'Why?' the man asked.

The doctor replied, 'I have finished your treatment.'

The man said, 'No, I have cured you.'

The doctor smiled. 'Sir, I pretended to be in pain only to cure you. Tell me, where is your pain now?'

It was gone. The man had forgotten about his pain while helping the doctor.

One often wonders why financial gain seems to benefit the most undeserving while the honest man is often poor. It is true that sometimes good people lack material comfort. But remember, inner peace is far more important than material comfort. Ambitious people can accumulate wealth but they do not have the inner wealth of peace, while a good-hearted person will never lack real happiness and peace.

Peace and disharmony are related to the leshya. If we understand the secret of leshya, all queries can be resolved. Money or financial status should not be the measuring stick of prosperity. Do not evaluate a person only according to his material wealth. There are other parameters as well.

Once, Lord Mahavir was asked, 'O Lord! Which is the most prosperous and which is the least prosperous soul in the world?'

Mahavir replied, 'The soul that has krishn leshya is the least prosperous. The soul with neel is a little better than krishn; the soul with kapot is better than neel; the soul that has tejo is better than kapot ; the soul with padm is better than tejo, and the soul that has shukla leshya is the most prosperous.'

Lord Mahavir evaluated a man by his spiritual wealth. If we all had this perspective we would have no stress or worry. Today, stress has become a trauma for many people. The reason for this is that we have limited perspective.

There are two perspectives – an outer perspective and an inner perspective. The outer perspective is concerned with the material world while the inner perspective is concerned with your thoughts and conduct. If you stay in krishn, neel or kapot leshya, you gain the world but lose your soul. Your outer environment gains riches while your inner world becomes poor. You will always feel that something is lacking in your life. You will not have complete peace. You will feel spiritually poor. If you want to be truly rich, strengthen your inner self.

An interesting capacity of colour is that it can take you from the outer to the inner world. As long as krishn, neel and kapot leshya are at work, you cannot move inward, you cannot become spiritual, and you cannot realize inner happiness. To strengthen your inner self, meditate on bright colours.

The next question is: How do I meditate on colours? In preksha meditation, once your mind achieves a state of no thought, you experience subtle vibrations. Eventually, your mind gets connected with the taijas body, and you begin visualizing colours.

RED

The colour of tejo leshya is the colour of the rising sun. Red is a constructive colour. It is the source of activity, strength, radiant glory and alertness. It also indicates good health. A doctor checks for red blood cells in the body as a sign of good health. Deficiency of red makes a person sick. Red is the sign of defence. The colour activates the nervous system and blood circulation. It stops outer toxins and unwanted contaminants.

When you activate your centre of intuition you can see the colour of tejo leshya in this area. This is the moment of unique bliss. With the experience of this colour, your internal journey begins. When you visualize bright red, you get into deep meditation and your habits are transformed. The old habits, developed due to krishn, neel and kapot leshya, become ineffective in the presence of the bright red of tejo leshya.

YELLOW

Padm leshya is bright yellow. This is also a very powerful colour. Like red, it is warm. At the physical level, yellow helps strengthen the brain and nervous system. If a child is weak in studies and bad at memorizing things, his memory will improve if he is kept in a yellow room. If you meditate on the colour yellow for ten minutes every day, it can even improve your IQ.

The psychological effect of yellow is happiness. According to the science of colour, yellow is a symbol of happiness. It dispels sadness and gives you bliss. The Jain scriptures say that padm leshya increases our peace of mind and inner bliss. It develops the power of intuition. Here, intuition means realization or experience of the self. It controls illogical and irrational thinking.

So we can conclude that the colour yellow makes you joyful, develops your IQ and intuition, and strengthens and activates your brain and nervous system. If you focus on the centre of bliss (the heart), on the centre of purity (the throat) and on the brain with bright yellow colours, all evil habits are diminished and good habits take their place.

Red and yellow objects produce a lot of heat and energy. Even tejo leshya and padm leshya do so. When the energy reaches its highest level – when there is no room for more increment – shukla leshya helps cool the energy down. This is the state of *nirvana* or liberation.

Lord Mahavir was once asked, 'O Lord! Is the result of krishn, neel and kapot leshya always inauspicious?'

'Not necessarily,' Lord Mahavir replied. 'With these three leshya, thoughts can be positive as well as negative.'

The quality of a colour is relative. Neel leshya is purer than krishn and kapot is purer than neel. Krishn leshya is at the extreme end of impurity while shukla leshya is at the extreme end of purity.

Colours are neither good or bad independently. It depends on the intensity and brightness of the colour. Even white can be negative if it is dull. The three negative leshyas – black, blue and grey – can become positive in their effect if they are bright. Similarly, tejo, padm and shukla can be negative if they are dull.

Black is not always negative. It is the colour of security and protection. In the Jain tradition, tirthankars (prophets) are worshipped with black, along with other colours. Lord Vishnu is worshipped with black. In the Vedic culture, Lord Brahma is worshipped with red because red is the colour of creation. Lord Shiva is worshipped with white as he is considered the destroyer. The colour violet is also significant in the development of spirituality. It helps control a violent disposition.

Therefore, each colour has its own impact. Meditating on colour will help you gain peace of mind, purity of thought and an integrated personality.

ESSENCE

❖ The soul that has krishn, neel and kapot leshya can gain material comfort but might lack mental peace and inner happiness. On the other hand, if you have tejo, padm or shukla leshya, you will always be peaceful and balanced.

❖ If you stay in krishn, neel or kapot leshya, you gain the world but lose your soul. Your outer environment gains riches, but your inner world becomes poor. You should not aim to make your material existence a happy one; try to make your inner persona happy, prosperous and blissful.

❖ There are three tools to develop your inner self:
1) Preksha meditation
2) Bhavana
3) Colour meditation

❖ Meditating on bright colours, not dark colours, makes you peaceful.

❖ Tejo leshya is bright red. It is the source of activity, strength, radiant glory and alertness.

❖ When you focus on your centre of intuition and visualize bright red or the colour of the sunrise, you delve into deep meditation and your habits are transformed for the better.

❖ Padm leshya is bright yellow. Padm leshya increases the tranquility of mind, peace and inner bliss. It develops the power of intuition.

❖ If you focus on the centre of bliss (the heart), centre of purity (the throat) and the brain with bright yellow, all evil habits are diminished and good habits take their place.

❖ Shukla leshya is the purest and most perfect state of man.

9
Why Meditate?

Action helps to drive life and inaction helps to know the truth behind life. One who believes in doing can only run his life, he cannot get the facts of life. On the other hand, one who believes in not doing knows the truth of life and he runs his life as well. He who meditates does not give up activity, whereas a doer leaves meditation out of his life.

Why should you meditate? Why should you adopt inactivity? Why should you stop movement and become motionless and quiet?

You might wonder whether meditation causes laziness. People generally do not like to engage in physically strenuous work. So if you tell someone to stop working and sit quietly, perhaps you are making them more complacent through meditation. And some people might question you for taking them away from physical work or activity.

The question is that of physical activity. First of all, let me clarify these two opposing ideas: effort and non-effort, activity and inactivity. If you do not understand this, you will not understand the meaning of meditation.

Effort or activity refers to the action done to maintain and run one's life. People work to live a worldly and social existence till the end of their life. Inactivity or non-effort is to gain the truth of life. Activity serves your outer purpose, while inactivity serves your inner purpose. One who believes in action goes through life without understanding its essence. On the other hand, he who believes in inaction knows the truth of life. He knows how to live life and he runs his life successfully as well. A person who meditates does not give up activity, but a person who is constantly active does not meditate at all.

If you try to search for the truth of life, you attain the outer world too. Your 'within' drives the 'without', for action comes out of inaction; your efforts are driven by non-effort. The action that comes out of inaction is more powerful.

Action itself is impure. If your action is biased by action, it will always be impure. In daily life, if you want to get any work done there is a long chain of activity, whether physical, mental or verbal. For example, if you want to go shopping, how many physical, mental and verbal activities will there be? At first, you will have the desire for something. Then you will plan to get it, or perhaps you will ask someone to accompany you. After that you will go to the shop and start looking for what you want. In between there will be the dilemma of whether you actually like the object. Finally, you buy the item if you are satisfied. There is a long series from beginning to end that includes physical, mental and verbal activities. All these activities are driven by some kind of emotion. Therefore, worldly activity is always impure. Actions are always rooted in world-oriented, external and physical realms. The physical, outer world is not conscious and pure. So when your actions are influenced by other actions, you are coloured by an outer force.

But the fact is, activity is not the end but the means to run one's life. A person who meditates is also active, but performs worldly affairs with a different perspective. He accepts activities as something with instrumental value, not as the ultimate goal of life.

We live in a scientific world that is concerned with understanding the nature of matter and solving the mystery of its existence. Scientific research concludes that matter is the only subject of knowledge and that there is nothing beyond matter.

The truth is that there are two entities in this world: matter and non-matter. But science does not accept the existence of the soul or pure consciousness. This is because scientific research is done through material instruments, and material tools can only observe the material world. These tools cannot know the soul.

This is why people understand meditation only as a healing process or therapy to control and cure physical and mental problems (like stress). But meditation is not just stress therapy. While it does provide emotional balance, strengthens the immune system, slows the aging process and controls high blood pressure, its prime utility is as a tool for developing spirituality. Your true self becomes manifest only when the superficial contaminants have been eradicated from your life through meditation. The external effects of meditation degrade its inner value. For instance, physical health is one of the positive benefits of meditation but it is not the ultimate goal. I do not wish to undermine the value of good physical health but at the same time I wish to remind the reader of the value of the unchanging pure self or pure consciousness which is far more precious than life and death.

Therefore, correct your purpose. Meditation has a specific purpose, which is to know and to experience the existence of the self. Until you understand your own self, health problems are hard to solve. Health issues are not just related to the atmosphere, weather or germs. Health is also related to your self. A negative perspective also leads to ill health and is the cause of much misery. Once you know the truth, the pain goes. To know yourself is to uproot pain.

Imagine you want a tree to grow and flourish. What do you need to do? You need to take care of the roots and water them. If you water the leaves and flowers, the tree will never grow. Conversely, if you don't want the tree to grow, cutting its branches will not help. You will have to uproot it. Similarly, everything that constitutes our existence is in the root of being. Normally, we think only of the external world as having any effect on our lives. We do not think of the inner world. We like to be on the top floor of the building, not at its foundation. Yet, until we step on the foundation we cannot reach the destination.

The root of pain and problems is, in fact, the inner world. Death and disease are not painful in themselves; it is the impure inner consciousness that makes us sensitive to pain, and makes us fear it. If you know this truth, that pain and pleasure are simply products of the mind, you will never be unhappy.

A man was returning home after twelve years. Before going to meet his family, he stayed in a motel for the night. At midnight, a boy in a nearby room started crying. The man couldn't sleep. He called the hotel management and told them to move the boy to another room. The manager sympathized with the boy, and said that he was merely a child, and it would take some time for a doctor to come see him. But the man was very rich and he wanted to get the boy out at any cost. The manager grudgingly obliged and the boy was sent outside. Later that night, the boy died.

The next morning, the man asked about the boy and discovered that the boy was his own son, who had come to see him. Now the man was in unbearable pain.

The question is: Where did the pain come from? Was it because of the death? If death had brought the pain, the man would have felt a physical pain when the boy died. But he did not become miserable when the boy was sent away; he did not become sad when the boy died. He was in pain only when he realized it was his own son. So it was his own thoughts and not death itself that caused him pain.

It is the emotions of attachment and hatred that make you happy or unhappy. That is why a situation, object or incident is not the primary cause of misery. Pain and pleasure are the products of your conscious experience. An object might be a secondary cause but the root cause is your own emotion or consciousness.

The way we react to situation is important. For instance, you hear about lots of deaths around the world, but you are not affected by all of them. Only if the person who has died is known to you do you feel sad. The same incident can have three types of reactions: 1) you are neutral, 2) you are unhappy, or 3) you are happy. Pain and pleasure are reflections of the likes and dislikes of our mind. But we tend to blame external factors instead. This is the wrong perspective.

Until we change our perspective, we cannot be happy. And until we explore our selves, we cannot uproot pain.

You might ask: What is the right perspective?

Well, the right perspective is to free the mind from the emotions of love and aversion. Until your mind moves away from these two persuasions, your thinking cannot be properly aligned, regardless of whether you memorize the scriptures or not. You cannot realize the truth until you relinquish the feelings of attachment and hate. Without realizing the truth, you cannot have everlasting happiness.

This is the true aim of meditation: to know the knower, to know the perceiver and to know the self.

There is a complete process of meditation to know the inner self. The inner self can be categorized into two: 1) *gyata* or the 'knower self' and 2) *bhokta* or the 'enjoyer self'. These are two opposite states of the same consciousness. Meditation purifies a person's sensations, and makes him give up bhokta and realize gyata.

The question is, what is the difference between bhokta and gyata? Someone who encases external experiences in pain and pleasure and is engaged with the external world is bhokta. A person who is in touch with his inner world and a mere observer of the outer world is gyata. A gyata knows and observes a situation, but does not get involved. If there is only knowledge without bias, that knowledge is pure. In this state, you understand the true nature of the material world and consciousness.

If you have an opinion about an external situation, you are in a state of bhokta, which is a person's normal self most of the time. You do not acknowledge the object in its real form but see your perspective, which changes with your sensations.

In winter, you love the heater. But would you still like to use it during summer? Never. Now the heater is neither good nor bad in itself. It is your perspective that changes. An object is constant. Being good or bad is not the nature of the object. It is a projection of the mind.

Perceive the object without the distorting vision of emotions. Now your knowledge can truly come into focus. Once this happens, any situation can be isolated from the consciousness. You know the truth of the situation. So your conscious self will not get influenced by it.

How can you change your perspective? Through meditation. After meditation you will see everything in its pure form. Nothing will be lost. Matter and consciousness will both remain intact in their real forms. Meditation helps you distinguish matter as matter and your consciousness as consciousness. Through meditation you experience your soul's consciousness and your body as a physical manifestation.

Meditation helps us know an object in its true form. Matter is transitory and a person who meditates understands that material gains never last. But the soul is permanent. You can never change the defining characteristics of the soul or replace it with an object. For example, you can create a new hybrid species of apple by interbreeding two different species of apple. But you cannot change its true nature. The apple remains an apple; it does not become a rock or plastic. A living being can never become non-living and vice versa. You can never change the true nature of an object. Meditation is the process to know the true object, despite its external form.

Dr Erwin Schrödinger, a Nobel prize-winning (1933) physicist and theoretical biologist, wondered how many molecules it takes to make a living being, and what properties these molecules might possess. He questioned scientists' search for the ultimate unit of matter and the root cause of matter, whether it was conscious or unconscious.

What is consciousness? Does it exist? How can we correlate matter and consciousness? These should be the main issues of scientific research but, sadly, science is misguided in its attempt to substantiate existence through quantitative means.

Now the question is: How can you know the soul? Search for the truth on your own. Don't rely on scriptures and traditions alone. Until you search on your own, you cannot experience your soul. When the scriptures say that souls exist, it is merely a verbal truth. You experience your own soul only when you get into deep meditation and experience the pure consciousness. When you read the scriptures you gain intellectual knowledge, but when you meditate, the experience is through your consciousness. Let us suppose a child does not know the taste of sugar. When you tell him sugar is sweet, he stores the information in his head. When he tastes sugar after that, he experiences its sweetness. At first his knowledge was intellectual but later it became experiential.

Until we experience the soul we will only know an intellectual or imaginary soul based on the description in scriptures or from spiritual teachers. Words in scriptures are a reflection of the soul; words are not the soul. You might then ask: What is the worth of words? If you are not cognizant of the soul, reading will inspire you to inquire about the soul. Words can make you curious to experience what is real. Words are significant, but don't stop your journey there.

Meditation will take you out of the world of reflection into the world of experience; it will replace propositional knowledge with empirical knowledge. By listening carefully within and remaining still until action is called forth, we can perform valuable, necessary and long-lasting service to the world while cultivating our ability to perceive the soul. Meditation will help you stop living your life in the shadow of an image.

Once there was an auction of paintings by great artists. One of the items for sale was a lively portrait of a poor but intriguing woman. The auction started and the painting sold for Rs 50,000. When the buyer left the auction house, he carried the picture with him. At the door he found a lady begging. It was the lady in the painting. He did not assist her in any way. What an irony it was! He spent 50,000 rupees on the painting but he could not spend a single rupee for the real lady who had been portrayed in the painting. In the same way, if you do not take the time to experience your own self, and are engaged in understanding it only at the intellectual level you are ignoring the real self in favour of the superficial self.

Therefore, practise meditation. Your sense of limited individuality will fade, and the supreme truth of the real self will become clear.

ESSENCE

✤ You need to meditate…
- to reveal the truth, to realize the pure consciousness and to know the knower.
- to stay aware and conscious and to unwind the materialistic bonding.
- to awaken the inner vision.
- to awaken the psychic centres.
- to transform the leshya and to strengthen and purify the aura.
- to make the conscious mind pure, aware, strong and inward.
- to be free of misery.

✤ Activity depletes energy. Inactivity secures and builds up energy.

✤ Memory, analysis and decision – these are the functions of the cerebellum, which can be enhanced through meditation.

✤ When the scriptures say souls exist, it is a verbal truth. As you get into deep meditation and you experience the pure consciousness, you experience your own soul.

✤ A meditator remains internally aware while engaging with the external world, for his action comes out of non-action. He is not attached to the material world. He is not driven by his senses and desires. He remains balanced.

10
Stress and Meditation – I

Science has provided us with many comforts but it is unable to give us peace.
It does not have a tool that releases stress. When we focus on philosophy, it
seems capable of freeing us from stress. Philosophy vitalized by spirituality and
experience can bring peace.

We practise meditation to reach the truth. The truth can be reached in two ways – either through logic or through experience and self-realization. There are two ways to know an object – either through reasoning or without reasoning. The objective world can be categorized into the gross and the subtle. The gross object can become the subject of our senses, mind and intellect. Such objects can be explained through logic. On the other hand, subtle objects cannot be perceived through our senses, mind or intellect. Hence they cannot be experienced physically. The subtle world can be experienced by our consciousness through meditation.

In the middle ages, logic and reasoning started to dominate philosophical theories and it was believed that truth cannot be understood without reason. Philosophy and logic became synonymous. But the shore of an ocean is not the ocean. The gems are found in its depths. In the same way, the depth of philosophy cannot be measured by logic. Gross aspects can be understood empirically. But the subtle facts are the subject of experience. It requires practice to comprehand them. But we have become entangled in logic and have overlooked the significance of self-realization and meditation.

Today, science is successful in its accounts of combining logic and experiment. Science and philosophy are not that different. It was philosophy that gave birth to science. When I started the practice of meditation, I realized that philosophy is becoming just a set of words and theories. Once philosophers took away self-experience and experiment from philosophy, it stopped developing. This has prevented us from understanding the secrets hidden in ancient literature. I would like to share an example.

In Jain philosophy, plants are accepted as living organisms. It is a unique concept not found in other philosophies. The Agam says that plants also breathe, take food and have emotions like anger, hate, attachment, love, compassion, possessiveness, etc. The authors of the Jain scriptures were not just philosophers but self-realizers, meditators and perceivers. Therefore, they have explained the concept of plants on the basis of personal experience. It was not an intellectual exercise but experienced truth. Subsequent Jain philosophers lived in the age of logic, so they were bereft of experience and found it difficult to explain the subtle truths revealed in the scriptures.

Plants possess *mati gyan* (perceptual knowledge) and *shrut gyan* (verbal knowledge). Mati gyan is knowledge that is acquired through the senses. Shrut gyan is acquired through interpretation of words, objects or gestures. For example, if you hear the word 'fire', you

— 128 —

interpret its meaning as something hot and when you see fire, the word 'fire' is immediately used to define it. This interpretation is shrut gyan. Shrut gyan is helpful in communication. Communicating through speech, writing or gestures and understanding what is being communicated are both shrut gyan.

Jain philosophers in later years could explain the presence of mati gyan in plants because it pertained to the mind and sense organs. Plants do not possess all five senses, they possess one sense – touch. But the later philosophers could not accept the presence of shrut gyan in plants. They could not understand how communication was possible without vocal and hearing organs. Plants do not have any means to know the past and future, or to connect the present with the past and future. How, then, can they have shrut gyan?

The Jain scholars had to verify the existence of verbal knowledge, and they used logic to explain that while plants do not seem to possess verbal knowledge, they do have a vague form of it. The scholars illustrated that plants have the instincts of hunger, fear, sex, possession, anger, etc. But they denied in plants the ability to communicate because it was not verified. This was because of the scholars' lack of self-experience.

Today, even science has proved that while the language of plants might be different, they, like humans, communicate with each other. An experiment by scientists at Kyoto University in Japan showed lima bean plants sending out distress signals to protect themselves and warn neighbouring plants of an impending attack by spider mites. Instead of words and sentences, the plants emitted chemicals to get their message across.

Professor Richard Karban and other University of California researchers clipped the leaves of sagebrush plants to mimic insects eating their leaves. The plants released volatile chemicals (*methyl jasmonate*), which the wind carried to nearby tobacco plants. The tobacco plants must have sensed the chemicals because they increased production of a defensive agent that caused their leaves to taste vile to insects.

This communication between plants was experienced and known by omniscient sages in ancient times. Since it was discovered that plants have life, modern scientists have also started to research this aspect of plants. In his research on plant stimuli, Dr Jagdish Chandra Bose discovered that plants respond to various stimuli as if they had nervous systems those of animals.

Dr Cleve Backster, director of the Backster School of Lie Detection in San Diego, is best known for his experiments in bio-communication in plants by using a polygraph machine. He discovered that plants are extremely sensitive and can sense the subtle emotions and intentions of man, which even man cannot understand.

One day, Dr Backster accidentally cut his finger and it started bleeding. Soon after, the polygraph, which was attached to a plant, moved and showed sympathy. Dr Backster decided to examine this further and connected the polygraph to a tree. A gardener came and stood near the tree. There was no movement in the pointer of the polygraph. Next, a woodcutter came up with an axe. The tree started shivering and the pointer indicated fear. How did the tree know that the first man was a gardener and the next person a woodcutter?

Dr Backster noticed similar reactions when a physiologist from Canada came to meet him. She used to conduct experiments where she would dry trees and burn them and then record their weight. She had been conducting these experiments for a few months and as soon as she entered the laboratory, the pointers of the polygraphs started moving. Only when she left the room did the needles become stable, and the plants relaxed.

Plants have tremendous power to understand and sense human emotions. Humans and plants are both conscious; both have a life and a soul. The consciousness of man is developed with an advanced intellect and defined senses. On the other hand, plants don't have a mind, intellect or structure of sense organs. However, plants do possess a soul, which is the source of their knowledge. People know the world through their sense organs, while a plant knows the world through its entire body.

The Jain Agam elucidates it as *savvenam savve*. The consciousness or soul experiences the object through its atoms. The soul is comprised of innumerable conscious atoms. We do not see only through our eyes, and we do not think only with our brains. We can see through our whole body and think through any part of our body. For, consciousness is everywhere in the body. Acupuncturists have discovered about 700 psychic centres in the human body. The centres are primarily located in the brain but are also present in the thumbs and fingers. The pineal, pituitary and thyroid glands are directly connected with the hands and legs. Your body has tremendous power. Every single part of the body is capable of knowledge. Though our ears are the tools with which we hear someone who does not have ears can hear through his whole body. His body becomes more sensitive and helps him hear. In fact, by dividing their functions, we have limited the capacity of our organs. We are dependent on our ears alone to hear and have lost our extrasensory perception as a result. Sound is nothing but a group of waves. The one who recognizes the subtle vibrations or waves can hear or know more than an ordinary person because our ears can only hear sound waves between 20 Hz and 20,000 Hz while subtle vibrations have frequencies beyond this range.

It is said that when a Jain tirthankar spoke, the listeners would understand in their own language; it did not matter if they were human or animal. The sound produced by the tirthankars was a mental projection, not a verbal one. They communicated through a kind of vibration, which the listeners understood.

In ancient Jain literature there is a term called *sambhinn-shroto-labdhi*. It refers to one who is endowed with the power to perform any function with any sense organ. In this state, he does not need to hear with his ears or see with his eyes. His entire body functions like a sense organ.

Philosophy needs to focus on experience so it can guide science. You might ask: Why does science need guidance? While it is true that science has unfolded the hidden secrets of the visible world and discovered new facts, it is still unable to know the knower. Science cannot explain the soul. Once you know the soul and consciousness, you become aware of your attachment with the material world. Science lacks this capacity. If philosophy becomes powerful by involving experiments and reasoning, it can create a new dimension of science.

What is the universe? It is a collection of substances. In the language of set theory, we can say that the primary set is the universe, which is the set of many substances. Each substance is a subset of the universe. The set of living beings is one of the subsets. Every living being is an element of this subset. The set of living organisms is so big that it occupies every single point of space. There are innumerable living forms located at each point of space. Within my fingers too are many micro organisms.

Each living unit is alive due to its soul. Let us understand the soul of a living organism.

Every soul has a field of conscious vibrations around it. This field is a kind of flow that broadcasts the consciousness to the external world. There is one more flow that brings reactions from the outside to the inside. This reaction is karma, which comes from the external world through the activity of the mind, body and voice. This basically means that there are two flows – outflow and inflow. Outflow is the flow of consciousness, which decides our actions at the physical level, and inflow is the flow of the reactions. This cycle of action and reaction keeps moving because of the presence of *mohaniya karma*.

Our unknown world consists of consciousness and karma. This world is not clear to us. We try to experience it through preksha meditation. The physical, mental and verbal actions are driven by mohaniya karma, which deludes the consciousness and takes us away from the facts and truth of life. A drunkard cannot think rationally. Similarly, the consciousness biased by mohaniya karma cannot be rational. Mohaniya karma causes murchha (delusion). Mohaniya karma and murchha are both inexpressive. We do not feel them directly but can realize them through the outcome. Owing to murchha we tend to ignore our true existence of consciousness and believe that the body is real and not the consciousness. Consequently our entire focus goes to maintain the body and worldly pleasure. Murchha begets attachment and aversion. Attachment exists in two forms – superiority and.inferiority. Superiority builds ego in the form of 'I' and 'mine' and inferiority decreases self-confidence and self-esteem. Furthermore, murchha increases urges like revenge, jealousy, and others, which ultimately leads to stress, unbearable trauma and impure aura.

Freud accepted sex as a basic instinct of every single living being. What Jainism calls 'attachment' is synonymous to the sex of Freud. According to Freud, the unconscious is the source of our motivations, whether they are simple desires for food or for sex. Freud could not explain the cause of sex. The Jain scriptures, however, take it a step forward to argue that delusion is the cause of sex or attachment. The result of karma, bonded in the past, is the cause of delusion.

There is also an order of emotions. Attachment begets greed; greed begets deceit; deceit begets ego; and ego begets anger. The most perceptible attitude is anger. The ego is less apparent than anger. Deceit is less apparent than the ego. Greed is less apparent than deceit and attachment is less apparent than greed.

Attachment → Greed → Deceit → Ego → Anger

Certain emotions do not post any impression or effect on the body. They are part of our concealed or unknown world, which is out of our reach. This is how, while moving from the unknown to the known world, when we reach the level of anger, our consciousness creates a platform to manifest the emotion. We started our journey from the main substance, the universe, and arrived at the consciousness of anger. And the root cause of anger is attachment.

Once you understand the hidden world it becomes easier to cure stress through meditation. If you include practice, experiments and experience, your mind will be peaceful. This is because of experience, which gives you a better understanding of the cause and its solution.

Once you understand the hidden world it becomes easier to cure stress through meditation. If you include practice, experiments and experience, your mind will be peaceful. This is because of experience, which gives you a better understanding of the cause and its solution.

It is said that Lord Mahavir used to preach in *ardh magdhi*, an ancient Indian language. But the audience would understand his words in their own language. How did they understand him?

Until you attain control over your thoughts and sensations, it is hard to understand sound waves. Leshya is in the form of waves. One who understands leshya can understand waves. Normally, we understand waves if they are translated into the pattern of thoughts, images and finally into words. If you want to develop a better understanding of waves, you need to understand the world of leshya. You can have access to the world of leshya if you learn to control your thoughts and emotions. To gain control over emotions, you need to practise perception of breathing. Just focus on your breath. This is the technique to develop control. The more you practise, the more capable you are of understanding the language.

In the age of Lord Mahavir, would the common public, animals and birds have such capacity?

This is an interesting but complex question. As far as animals and birds are concerned, they have a tremendous capacity to understand vibrations. Animals are not dependent on their sense organs alone. They use their entire body to know. On the contrary, man is dependent on his sense organs. Man hears only through his ears while animals and birds hear through their entire body. Man has lost the ability to use his entire body. But a great yogi has such strong vibrations or energy that he can awaken or magnetize the dormant power of an ordinary man. When such power is awakened in an ordinary person, this power, in conjunction with the power of the meditator, helps him understand different vibrations.

A common question is whether it is necessary to keep the spinal cord straight while meditating.

The spinal cord is curved. But you need not worry about its structure while meditating. Just make sure your back is straight while sitting. The lotus posture is one of the best sitting postures for meditation, as it keeps your back straight. Similarly, *siddhasana* or the half-lotus posture also helps you sit straight. You should not bend. People tend to bend while sitting. Whenever people are told to sit straight they start complaining about back pain. Actually, sitting straight does not cause pain, it simply helps you to experience the pain that is already present. This pain is the result of bending your spinal cord when sitting. When you sit straight, it helps your consciousness travel straight through the spinal cord from the gyan kendra down to the shakti kendra and back up. When your consciousness makes such a trip, it controls your thoughts and your mind.

ESSENCE

- ❖ The new dimension of philosophy is to experiment and to experience.
- ❖ There are two ways to know an object – through reasoning and without reasoning.
- ❖ The objective world can be categorized into two: gross and subtle. The gross object can become the subject of our senses, mind and intellect. Such objects can be explained rationally. But the subtle cannot be perceived through physical means and hence cannot be explained through logic.
- ❖ The secrets of plant life are hard to reveal through empirical study.
- ❖ Plants have feelings, memories and the power of identification.
- ❖ Meditation can manage stress. Emotions or instincts are the creators of stress. Becoming aware of them helps you lead a stress-free life.

11

Stress and Meditation – II

The moment you start feeling attachment, stress has begun to manifest itself.
As soon as you connect with someone or something, you start focusing on
how it plays an integral part in your conception of well-being. The fear of
disconnecting from the object of your attachment is the root cause of stress.
Meditation helps you change the direction of your concentration and
correct the course of your consciousness in accordance with what is
healthy for your soul.

There are two worlds, known and unknown. We live in both, shifting from the known to the unknown and vice versa. Sometimes we live at the gross level, sometimes at the subtle level, and in both worlds we behave differently. When we shift from the unknown to the known world, we become social. When we are in the unknown world, we become introspective.

The unknown world is comprised of the karmic body, delusion and emotions. There is no external connection with this world. When we live at the karmic level, it is intra-personal. When we are within our spheres of emotion, we are enveloped by solace and seclusion. All three (karmic body, delusion, and emotion) are personal. When we cross the state of delusion and enter the state of attachment, we cling to the social life. The first step of social life is attachment. Stress and dependency within the social life are correlated. As long as you are at the personal level, you are solitary and stress does not bother you, so maintaining an emotional equilibrium is simple. But when you begin interacting socially and you get attached to others, stress comes to the forefront of your experience and begins to manifest itself.

However, without attachment you can never be social. Attachment creates a bond between two entities. When you get bonded, your social life starts. Not only does attachment connect man to man, it also connects man to matter. Without deception, the complex web of societies would not form and man would feel alone.

Once you get attached, the energy of attachment keeps flowing and begins to take on new forms. Eventually, the energy of attachment triggers greed. You begin to crave more and start accumulating possessions. The instinct of greed forces you to become hypocritical and you start deceiving. Without deception you cannot accumulate, because in order to secure your possessions you need to hide them.

In this way, attachment triggers greed, and greed triggers deceit. Next comes the ego. You are unaware of the way it slowly creeps into your life. When you attain wealth, your mind becomes prejudiced. You believe that all your wealth belongs to you. Now your ego forms. You compare yourself with others and begin to feel superior. This is how the impulse of accumulation disunites people. It splits society in two – superior and inferior. Without the inferior, there can be no superior. The ego needs someone to be lower than itself.

If there is no higher, no lower, no diversity, and all are equal, how can the ego grow?

The ego gives birth to anger. If someone you have deemed your possession does not listen to you, you get angry. If you are not attached to the person, you don't react to this. Why is there a difference? It is due to expectations. You expect your friends and family to listen to you. If it does not happen, your ego is wounded and you get angry. It is the ego that fuels anger.

Anger is a symptom of the core of your personality, for it shows what you are.

～

The factors affecting our social relations are attachment, greed, crookedness and ego. These factors are responsible for stress. The moment you start feeling attachment, stress has begun to manifest itself in its embryonic stage. As soon as you get connected to someone, you start focusing on how this person plays an integral role in your conception of well-being. This is the beginning of social life. Once you get attached, you keep thinking of that object or person and are scared of getting disconnected from it. This is stress. Let us analyse the mechanism of stress.

In the first stage you feel attachment. Attachment brings craving or greed. Later, greed creates fear of separation. Fear is the biggest contributing factor to stress. It works because of the force of attachment. You are scared of losing the object – your body, family, or your property. The fear of loss makes you focus on material things even more.

～

We all meditate – not just spiritual people, but children and elders, men and women. Meditation is not just practised in an ashram or in a meditation camp. You have actually been doing meditation for a long time in your home.

Simply, meditation is to concentrate. At home you focus on certain issues. But that focus is biased by attachment and fear. This kind of meditation is known as *arta dhyan* (focusing energy to get the object) and *raudra dhyan* (focusing energy to protect the object). In this, your concentration is fixed on attaining and preserving an object. You think of ways to acquire more material things and then focus on securing the objects. Day and night, awake or asleep, you think of the material world.

Preksha meditation, on the other hand, is the way to focus within. It is done while you are consciously awake, and away from the material world. You do it intentionally and willingly. While arta dhyan and raudra dhyan happen involuntarily, preksha meditation needs concentration. We all have this power of concentration by default, so you cannot say that it is hard for you to concentrate or that your concentration is weak. I believe you can focus thoroughly. But, at present, the object of your meditation is the material world. The objective of a meditator is to discover what is within himself. That is the basic difference between a meditator and you.

You need to learn meditation to change the direction of your concentration. You need to learn meditation to correct the course of your consciousness in accordance with what is healthy for your soul. The previous path was focused on the outer world; now you need to focus on the inner world. This is the only aim of learning preksha meditation, to shift the energy that is flowing towards attachment to your own existence.

Once Lord Mahavir was asked, 'O Lord! What is the benefit of having faith in spirituality?'

Lord Mahavir replied, 'By having faith in spirituality you get detached from the material world. When you get detached from one thing, you can get attracted to another.'

When you stop being attracted to the material world then you can enter the spiritual one. Inversely, when you start exploring spirituality, you will start ignoring the material world. It means you live in the material world, doing worldly activities, but you are aware of what you are doing. And you are engaged in the world to survive, not to eat, drink and be merry. Your activities are in moderation. You will be content, and live simply. You do not hate the world, but are a mere observer. You fulfil your duties but stand apart, just like the lotus. A lotus stays pure and clean even though it lives in the mud. Likewise, the perspective of a spiritual person towards the world will be quite different. When the external world is no longer appealing, your attention shifts to the inner world. If the flow of interest goes to one field, then the other contradictory field will automatically get disconnected. It's up to you to decide where you wish to aim your interest. I would suggest you take the energy of your interest towards your consciousness. The more attached you are to the material world, the more stressed you will be. You get stressed because of your interest and attraction to the material world. You are not interested in your own true self. It is your focus that is both cause and antidote for stress. and can cure stress. When the focus of your intention is concentrated on attaining and preserving a material object, stress is inevitable. When your focus goes within to experience the inner world, you are relieved of stress.

⌒

Arta dhyan and raudra dhyan make your leshya impure. Your leshya becomes black and grey and your aura and emotions also become impure. When your emotions become impure, your mind follows suit. An impure mind generates impure thoughts. When your thoughts are impure, your behaviour also becomes impure. When your behaviour becomes impure, your social relationships get disturbed. Your entire life is disrupted.

Then you start thinking of ways to solve your problems. You want to change your life. You want to turn back. When you turn back and look within, you realize it is a negative attitude (irritation or anger) that is bothering you. One person's behaviour hurts the ego of a second person. The behaviour of the second hurts the ego of the third. In this way, dislike and hate increase.

For example, if your boss is upset with you, you get upset. You come home and get angry with your spouse. Now your spouse is upset. He or she gets angry with your child. Your child also gets upset. The whole atmosphere becomes negative, influenced by one person.

The main reason for this is attachment, which is the root cause of hate. Attachment and hate are two seemingly different emotions, but they are, in fact, not. If you do not have attachment, you cannot have hate. When you are away from your true self, you get attached to the material world. Attachment leads to greed, greed leads to dishonesty, which leads to ego, and finally ego leads to anger. There is no hate in this chain. So, where does the hate come from?

When you are attached to an object or a person, you become greedy and to satisfy your greed you start deceiving others. When you are met with an obstacle, you start disliking that person, because your ego is hurt. If you only felt positive emotions, you would have the same love for everyone with no discrimination. Hate is a necessary emotion to acknowledge this difference. Anger and ego are the manifestations of hate.

Love is converted to hate when it is connected with the ego and anger. When you sense an obstacle to the object that you like, you begin to dislike it. This means that dislike or hate is simply an obstacle to your attraction. It does not have an independent existence, so do not try to eliminate it. The thing you have to get rid of is attachment. This is the beginning, the focal point of your awakening. Do not misunderstand this concept. Do not think that if you meditate, if you divert your energy from arta dhyan and raudra dhyan to the inner world, you will be completely disconnected from the outer world. It is not so. Does a meditator not live family life? Does he not eat and drink? Does he not wear clothes? Does he not buy a house? Does he not feed his family? He does.

All meditators do not become monks or sages. Even a sage needs things to live – food, clothes etc. How can one live without basic necessities? There is no hatred for the material world. To stay detached is not to hate and run away from one's duties. If someone starts hating material things, abuses them, says negative things about the material world, then he is not spiritual but mentally disturbed. You cannot leave the material world; you have to change your attitude towards it.

Whoever comes to a meditation camp does not come to leave the material world. If this were the case, their families would never allow them to come.

You attend meditation camps to change your perspective, to see the material world without the colour of good or bad, love or hate.

Relaxation alone cannot make you spiritual. Merely sitting in a lotus posture does not change the flow of energy. You can sit in the lotus posture and plan to kill someone. The change in direction takes place when you have the right perspective.

Matter was, is and will for ever be in the world. Socialism brought about the concept that wealth is not a personal property, it belongs to society. I personally believe that this concept is correct to an extent. Man believes that money is his personal property. Socialists believe that individual ownership of wealth is harmful for society and that an individual cannot own wealth, because wealth is not the property of an individual but that of society.

A man with the right perspective will say that wealth belongs neither to an individual nor to society. To perceive an object as 'mine' is a delusion. Spirituality says neither man nor society owns property. It is its own entity. Matter belongs to matter.

A Sanskrit poet once described the earth as a girl who can never get married. Many kings, emperors and rulers say that they rule a particular part of the land, that they own the land. But it is merely an illusion. Nobody can own land. People come and go, they cannot take their land with them.

Individual possessions create inequality and thus trouble in society. There is no solution for such troubles. Therefore, some people believe that there should be trusteeship and not ownership. But this is not a complete solution for it generates new problems. Until you correct the fault, you cannot troubleshoot the problem. Until one understands that matter is matter, and that it does not belong to anybody, there will be immorality and dishonesty. Matter and the individual are separate entities. You can be in a relationship with an object and with an individual, but there should not be any craving for the object. You must see matter as a utility, to be employed for a purpose. Do not get attached to it. Do not experience a union with it. This is the state of a 'knower'.

~

The first step to cure stress is to become an observer. The second step to cure stress is bhavana. We are all attached to matter. When you look at an object, you can get so hypnotized that you lose self-control. Autosuggestion can help us to be conscious of our own self. The greatest power of bhavana is the power of knowledge. You can realize the power of your knowledge through practice.

At the beginning of the practice, recite the arham sound. You energize yourself with arham. Eventually, this is what you will start feeling: *I have infinite knowledge, intuition, energy and bliss within me. I do not need any other bliss. I cannot attain bliss in the material world. I am full of bliss. I am complete.* If you bond with this infinity, if you get empowered by it, then your bonds with the physical world will be eliminated. The transitory loses its power in the presence of the infinite. This is how autosuggestion brings about change and cures stress. The third step to cure stress is *vichay dhyan* or analytical meditation. Preksha is self-analysis. You analyse yourself through questions: *Why do I get angry? Why am I greedy? Why is my perspective wrong?* Negative emotions arise when you do not analyse. When you self-analyse, your knowledge-power is awakened. A person who does not use his knowledge-power develops a mind that is distorted by negative energies. Therefore, critically analyse yourself. As you begin analysing, arta dhyan and raudra dhyan are left behind and you enter dharma dhyan, the pure inner world. This is a healing process.

Modern psychologists treat their patients with the help of analysis of the inner world. First, the psychologist lets the patient relax. Then he asks his patient to reveal every incident of the past without hesitation and analyse it. The psychologist listens to him and understands how the problem started, what type of emotional or mental problem it is, and what emotions the patient has suppressed. Later, he heals the patient through hypnosis by giving suggestions followed by self-hypnosis where the subject gives auto-suggestions.

Spiritual healing works in the same way. Arta dhyan and raudra dhyan create physical and psychological problems, and you should not suppress the emotions caused by these. Suppression can lead to psychosomatic diseases. But it is imperative that you do not stop here. Understand this concept in the spiritual language. Release the negative energy. Do this not by expressing the negative emotion but by expressing a positive emotion. If you do not counteract negative emotions, the emotions are reinforced, and the cycle of negative energy repeats itself. Suppose you are angry and you want to express it. You show your anger with harsh words, and once the feeling is expressed, you think that the anger is gone and it will never come back. This is a fallacy. It is absent at the physical level, but before leaving the body it leaves its impression in the form of energy or atoms. This energy remains inside you, causing you stress. If you really want to get rid of your stress, you will have to learn to release negative energy, purify it, and thus control your anger.

If social life begins with attachment, does a completely detached person (veetrag) not have a social life?

A detached soul does not live like a social man. He lives at the individual level. Veetrag refers to a person who stays in society but is completely detached from it. Like a veetrag, a spiritual ascetic also lives a detached life. Acharya Bhikshu, founder of the Terapanth sect of Jainism, said, 'Even while living in a religious group or order, an ascetic should not be attached to any person.' A true spiritual is disconnected from worldly life.

Lord Mahavir emphasized this when he said, 'Man! You empower yourself with this feeling that, after all, you are alone.'

Man enters the worlds alone and leaves it alone. Nothing comes or goes with him. He performs actions independently and attracts karma and he alone enjoys the fruit of his karma. No one shares this with him.

Matter is matter and man is man. If there is no mutual relationship between these, how can society move?

If this happened, society would be at peace and there would be no trouble. Let's put it this way: You are hungry and you need food to eat. So you think: *I need food to satisfy my hunger. Food and hunger are two different issues. Food is a necessity, not my desire.* If you develop such a view, you will not eat more than necessary. You will not crave food. But if you get attached to food, you have a different view. You will think: *I like it. This is my favourite dish.* Then you will not take care of your hunger, health and need; you will eat to fulfil your desire, not to satisfy your hunger.

We do not need objects to satisfy our desire. Objects are there to fulfil our needs and to run our life. If we use matter only when necessary, there will be no problem.

We do not need to wipe out the material world, we need to disconnect our attachment with it. Jain monks do not keep money.

They keep the things they really need. They keep books that might be worth millions of rupees. But they are not attached to them and do not possess them.

Perceive matter, consciousness and man from a different angle. Each is useful to the others. This viewpoint makes for a healthy society. I am not saying that matter is not worthwhile. Material things are useful. It is not attachment to them that runs social life peacefully, but it is the feeling of usefulness that makes social life easy and peaceful.

ESSENCE

- The main cause of stress is arta dhyan and raudra dhyan. Arta dhyan means focusing your energy to attain the material object. Raudra dhyan means focusing your energy to protect the object.

- Stress begins with the emotions of attachment, greed and desire.

- Fear begins with the thought that you will soon be disconnected from the things you feel possessive of.

- Attachment begets hate for others; hate begets ego; ego begets anger.

- To stay away from stress, practise being a knower and perceiver. Do not get involved in the event.

- Go in search of consciousness. Find the place of consciousness and the soul.

- Do not suppress anger, fear and other emotions; erase them.

12

The Secret of Aura

Every human being has a physical aura (abha mandal) and a psychical aura (bhav mandal). Our consciousness activates our bioelectric body which then radiates electrostatic rays. The rays envelop the entire body, and form an oval shape around it. This is known as the physical aura. The quality of the physical aura depends upon the quality of the psychical aura. By changing the conscious energy through meditation, one can change the physical aura.

It is hard to find a personality that consists of the trinity of strength, higher consciousness and bliss. Animals are very strong but they cannot use their strength as a sentient life form due to their dormant consciousness. Man uses his strength in a more strategic manner because he has a developed consciousness. Without developing the consciousness, one cannot use strength. For example, lions, elephants, bulls and buffaloes are very powerful, but they use their strength without higher thought. There are two ways of using the strength of animals; it is used by man or for the animal's own instinctual purpose, which is mainly predatory.

Whenever I see bullocks in India carrying loads, I think they would not be beasts of burden if they had developed a higher consciousness. They have been doing the same work for thousands of years and will do so through the existence of the species. There is no change, no transformation. All periods, all ages are the same for them; it does not matter whether they lived in the stone age, medieval age or atomic age.

Because of his developed consciousness, man needs only minor physical effort to control more powerful animals and to use their strength for his own needs. Thus, the saying goes: He who is endowed with intelligence has the greatest strength. The power of intelligence, consciousness and knowledge can beat physical strength.

Even if you have strength and intelligence, you are still missing one important thing – bliss. You use your strength but, unfortunately, you do not use it properly. Only someone who has a developed consciousness combined with a knowledge of the proper use of physical strength can experience inner bliss. Animals do not have the potentiality of a developed mind due to their dormant consciousness, so they can't possibly direct their strength to achieve higher consciousness. But man can. If you know how to regulate your consciousness, and where to use it, you can experience bliss.

You can attain bliss through meditation. You can regulate your consciousness in such a way that your energy flows in the right direction. The right energy can make you feel blissful. But when your energy does not flow in the right direction, your bliss gets destroyed.

Energy works everywhere. Without energy there is no anger, no ego, no attachment, no love, no sexual desire and no lust. No task can be done without energy. Those who believe in God as a creator of this world say that nothing can happen in this world without God. But I say that nothing can happen without energy.

It is amazing that energy can manifest itself through many processes in very distinct ways. It is like electricity. Electricity is the same throughout your house, but when it supplies power to the refrigerator or AC, it cools and when it is transmitted to the heater, it gives heat. Electricity is neither hot nor cool; it is a force that activates the system. Similarly, if your vital energy goes to the place that activates anger, your anger is awakened; when energy goes to the sexual centre, sexual desires are activated. You have both positive and negative centres of energy. The centre the energy hits gets activated and the corresponding attitude comes into effect.

Now the question is: How can one stop negative attitudes? There is no unanimous answer to this. Some people say that you should not repress your emotions, while others argue that you should suppress them.

The first concept says that if you are angry, you should express it. Once you have allowed your rage to peak, the anger will not come back. If you experience any emotion at its highest level, the emotion ultimately gets uprooted. Another theory gives emphasis to suppression. If you are angry, don't say anything, do not express yourself. If you have sexual desires, don't attempt to satiate them.

Man is social. He lives in social environments. One relatively undesirable aspect of this is group conformity. Society has its own system of discipline and code of conduct. There are certain obligations that society wants you to maintain. It does not allow you to be too liberal. Society establishes some basic ground rules, which say: Suppress your negative behaviour. You are a social man, you live in a group, so you have to control yourself. You cannot do whatever you want. This is how social systems introduced the theory of suppression and developed discipline and punishments codified by laws. Laws were introduced and developed by society and the state. The state cannot allow you to extend your personal rights to the detriment of others. Discipline is expected to produce a specific character, self-control or a pattern of behaviour, especially aimed at moral or mental improvement. Whoever crosses the line falls into disfavour. So, there is one basic rule of social management: control yourself or be ready to face the consequences.

The second concept supports expression. This is a concept that is accepted by a relatively small number of people. They believe that if you control your desires and don't fulfil them, these suppressed desires get accumulated, and over time they manifest in a way well beyond the ability of a person to control them. So this concept asserts that you shouldn't suppress your emotions; instead you should express yourself freely. Supporters of this concept concluded that the suppression of attitude can have a negative effect. Suppose you are very aggressive and you feel as though you want to explode. If you suppress your anger, you can end up with an unbearable headache. This stress can have a negative effect on your heart as well. So a suppressed attitude can make you physically and mentally sick. Therefore, it is advisable never to suppress one's desires and emotions.

I agree with this concept. But to express and enjoy your desires beyond the limits of moderation is not good. It has a negative effect on society. The problem is that the concept of 'do not suppress' was interpreted as 'uncontrolled enjoyment'. Many spiritual leaders have advocated uncontrolled sensual and sexual enjoyment in the name of spirituality. Today, western societies are generally against this form of hedonism while the Indian social system has never accepted it.

Freud was never in favour of suppression; he would prefer sublimation or transformation. Even spirituality, to an extent, supports the concept of 'do not suppress'. Normally, not suppressing should mean sublimation and transformation of attitude. When I apply this to spirituality, I find that while psychology can advise you to transform or channelize your sexual attitudes, spirituality cannot. In spiritual language, you can only erase sexual desire. The atoms and energy of sex and anger cannot be transformed into other forms. They can only be destroyed. The problem is that we have sub-categorized energy into the energy of anger, the energy of sex, the energy of ego, and so on. But energy is one; it does not have qualities like anger or ego. The function of energy is to activate the system. If energy flows to the sexual centre, this centre will be activated. If energy goes towards the centre of anger, anger will become effective. And if energy goes towards forgiveness, the attitude of forgiveness comes into effect. The manifestation of the energy depends on how and where it is directed.

To accept the transformation of sexual desire is to accept sexual desire as an eternal habit. But sexual desire is not permanent. It is a molecular configuration that veils the true nature of our pure consciousness. We can erase those molecules but we cannot transform them. If you want to change a habit, you can do so by changing the direction of your energy flow. It is not the transformation of the energy but diversion of the flow of energy that results in the change. If you want to transform sexual desires, don't let the energy go where it will cause this activation; change the direction of your energy in a positive direction. The resultant leshya or attitude will make your aura pure.

WHAT IS AURA?

Every human being has a physical aura (*abha mandal*) and a psychical aura (*bhav mandal*). The physical aura is an analogous atomic configuration while the psychical aura is our consciousness. Our consciousness activates our bioelectric body. The active bioelectric body radiates electrostatic rays, which envelop the entire body, forming an oval shape around it. This is known as the physical aura. The quality of the physical aura depends upon the quality of the psychical aura. If the psychical aura is pure, the physical aura will be pure. If the psychical aura is impure, the physical aura will also be impure, dark, dull and distorted. Kashay makes the psychical aura impure. In an impure aura, all the bright colours are wiped out. But by changing our conscious energy, one can change the physical aura. In fact if our thoughts are positive and benevolent the aura will also be the same. The effect of positive aura can be seen on our physical organs also. When our thoughts are negative our physical organs get them dull colour spots on them. This is why diseases can be identified earlier if the aura is read. Therefore, to keep your aura pure and to stay healthy, have positive thoughts and change the direction of your energy from negative to positive.

So, of the three views on dealing with one's emotions – suppression, enjoyment and release – Jain philosophy is in favour of release. If you get angry, don't suppress it. If you try to suppress it, the energy struggles to come out. Eventually, the organ it impacts gets harmed and the mind too is damaged. So don't suppress the energy. Instead, release the energy through meditation and autosuggestion.

> When you start feeling angry, just say some pleasant words. The sound waves of the words, autosuggestion and long breathing help release the energy of anger. While exhaling, along with the internally generated carbon dioxide, the anger also leaves your body.

When the instinct of sex is stimulated and the energy gets released, you feel satisfied and good. But why do you feel good? When the bio-energy gets connected to the sex initiators, your sexual desires are stimulated. When you fulfil your desire, the energy is released and you feel relaxed and happy. If it remains inside, it makes you uncomfortable. Similarly, an aggressive person finds peace when he says what is on his mind. If he wants to fight, he feels satisfied after he has fought.

Is this real happiness? Is it beneficial? No, it isn't. While releasing negative energy you are also depleting your positive energy. You become empty; you lose your patience and intelligence; your creativity slows down; your physical, mental and intellectual powers diminish. The fuel of energy that keeps your vital energy active is depleted.

This is what you get when you fulfil your negative instincts. So don't waste your energy; delete the atoms of negative attitude and preserve your energy.

⌒

No guru has explained the idea of suppression. Spiritual science does not support it. The one who is omniscient, devoid of kashay, endowed with the right perspective, who has understood the soul and practises deep spirituality, is a true guru. Acharya Rajneesh condemned certain gurus because their religions teach suppression. But religion never teaches suppression. It talks of eradication.

Religious leaders teach the process of eradication. Eradication and inhibition should both be managed in such a way that old karma is eradicated and the new cannot enter. When eradication and inhibition take place, positive energy increases because negative energy decreases. When positive energy increases, the aura becomes pure and positive too.

To make our energy positive we must give up negative instincts. But before doing so, we need to understand negative attitudes and how various negative instincts impact our energy, body and daily life.

⌒

The process of transformation explained by psychology fits into one particular social system. It does not make us spiritual. Spiritual science defines a process that can discard the old attitude and awaken a new consciousness, a new personality.

Instinct is a powerful natural impulse. When old bonded karma, along with conscious vibrations, reach the leshya, the vibrations take the gross form as the instinct. This rising instinct incites the corresponding gland. The gland discharges the hormone and the person feels the urge of that rising instinct at mental and physical levels. For example, when the impulse of sex incites the genitals and gonads, you feel sexual desire. Similarly, the arousal of the impulse of anger or fear stimulates the adrenal glands and makes you feel angry or fearful.

When energy moves around the navel the attitude of anger, fear and sex is intensified. An intense attitude upsets the equilibrium of a person and makes the aura impure. The energy that flows down to activate the attitude needs to move upward to the centre of knowledge instead.

Just as a crystal reflects the colour that surrounds it, your leshya changes with your emotions and your aura changes according to your leshya. The theory of leshya says that krishn leshya gets converted to neel; neel becomes kapot; kapot becomes padm; padm becomes tejo; and finally tejo becomes shukla.

You can change your attitude by changing your leshya. Through this process you can rectify and purify the sexual centre too. You can cleanse all these malevolent centres so that even when the instincts of anger and sex arise inside as waves, the centres are not activated and the instincts are not manifested at the physical plane. When the centres are purified, a magnetic field is produced around them, which restricts negative attitudes. The instinct which arises at the inner level is not able to stimulate the centre at the physical level, because the instincts are destroyed before they can affect the body. Consequently, the attitude disappears.

This is possible only through the upward flow of energy. When your energy goes to the upper centre of the body, all negative attitudes get eradicated. The thyroid, Adam's apple, pituitary gland, pineal gland, vishuddhi kendra, darshan kendra, jyoti kendra and shanti kendra are the upper centres of the body. The energy flows upwards and activates these centres. When these centres are activated, they activate the hormones of the corresponding gland, which are positive in nature, and purify the attitude by removing the impulse. In this way, the impulse becomes ineffective before the arousal of the instincts. For, the direction of the energy is changed before it can incite the corresponding organ and gland. Consequently, the aura is pure.

The primary purpose of meditation is to reverse the flow of energy and make it flow upwards. If you do not know how to change the direction of energy, you will either express your instinct or suppress it. The practice of meditation, chanting and other spiritual practices like fasting, swadhyay, etc. are techniques to uplift energy.

If you have a headache and someone massages your head, you immediately feel relaxed. If you have pain anywhere in your body and external pressure is applied, the pain goes away. This is the magic of vital energy. If the vital energy of one person comes in contact with the vital energy of another person, he feels soothed. Remember, this is only healing; it is not a spiritual practice. Such techniques can cure physical problems. By injecting vital energy and coming in contact with others, you can cure mental frustrations and also release suppressed desires. Think of a man who hates another person. Through pranic healing he can be free of his hate for that person and build a new relationship with him. But this technique is incomplete. It might remove hate for one person but the emotion of hate is not gone completely. It is still present. Therefore, this process does not purify your aura permanently.

In ancient India, Sthulbhadra, son of Shakdal, a prime minister, did not enjoy the company of girls. His father could not understand this behaviour. He wanted his son to get married. So he sent his son to the famous prostitute, Kosharupa. Shakdal asked her to make Sthulbhadra attracted to girls by using her skills. Kosharupa succeeded and Sthulbhadra started taking an interest in girls and a sexual life. His hatred of woman was now gone.

Was this a spiritual experiment? Was it the practice of meditation? Kosharupa treated Sthulbhadra psychologically but that does not make it a spiritual practice. These days, in the name of spirituality and meditation, some hermitages use sex aids to cure the distress of both men and women. People who are afraid of interacting with the opposite sex are treated through sexual discourse. They call this a meditation technique but it is only an effort to develop the business of sex in the name of meditation. Such techniques might cure psychological problems but they are certainly not spiritual or meditation techniques.

I am emphasizing the instinct of sex and anger because these two instincts are stronger and more apparent in people. These instincts make our aura impure. In turn they lead to other negative emotions like fear, attachment, hate, greed, etc. During the sexual act, energy moves towards the lower part of the body, thereby activating intense lust and desires through the genitals. Moreover, more energy is consumed during the sexual act because of intense desire. Consequently, the level of vital energy goes down.

To keep the aura pure, one needs to discipline and regulate the urge of instincts, which ultimately stores energy in its pure form. Meditation, by connecting you with the inner world, can help you achieve this.

ESSENCE

✤ The purpose of meditation is to develop an integrated personality endowed with strength, higher consciousness and bliss.

✤ Through meditation you can regulate your consciousness in such a way that your energy will flow to make you blissful.

✤ When your energy goes to the upper centres of the body, your negative attitudes are eradicated.

✤ The flow of vital energy manifests two distinctly different human capacities – sex and knowledge. The former is natural and the latter is acquired. This is the difference between man and animal.

✤ In opening yourself to new ways, don't suppress sex or attachment but awaken and experience the higher consciousness.

13

Aura and Awakening of Power – I

In his search for truth, man becomes powerful. But stress makes him powerless.
The more he stresses, the greater his sexual desire becomes. Such a person has a
black aura. Therefore, awaken your power through meditation by
changing the leshya.

We all want to be enlightened. There are two types of light: the light of the soul and the light of taijas. We move constantly between the two.

The light of the soul glows but it does not show. This light is everlasting. Interestingly, this light does not need any fuel. It glows perpetually through its own power.

The light of taijas is the light of our body. During meditation, people sometimes experience colour flashes and sparks. These sparks and flashes are products of the taijas sharir or bioelectric body and are occasionally visible to the meditator.

There are numerous obstacles to the attainment of enlightenment. These obstacles are your own attitudes. You have accumulated attitudes that appear from time to time, sometimes in the nervous system and sometimes in the psychical centres, in the form of waves. These waves stimulate the muscular system. When muscles get stimulated they translate into behaviour. Consequently, your spiritual practice of enlightenment gets disturbed. To prevent this from happening, you need to train yourself so that those waves do not come up. Even if you cannot obstruct the surge of generated waves, the muscular system should be trained not to get stimulated by them. So practise meditation for the purification of the muscular system. Practise for the purification of your attitudes and impressions. Spiritual practice opens the new doors of the inner world, closing the doors of innate instincts.

Innate door		Acquired new door
Sex	→	Celibacy
Stress	→	Relaxation
Thoughts	→	Thoughtlessness
Noise	→	Silence
Outer electric vibrations	→	Inner electric vibrations

The major obstacle to be overcome spiritual practice is *rag* or attachment. And the ego is the strongest representative of attachment when it is revealed in the form of rage, fear and lust.

Though we may practise austerity, until we achieve it the attitude swings from positive to negative and vice versa. When you experience the feeling of being attacked or offended, you become irritated, frustrated and angry right away. This rage can be momentary, short-term, long-term or lifelong. Sometimes you feel sexual impulses that may be caused by a memory or an incident. This, of course, takes you off the spiritual path. The impulse of fear is always there – the fear of accidents, failure, getting insulted, losing wealth or status and many more. Every day you face these impulses many times. You take a few steps forward in spirituality but your impulses pull you back. And until you get rid of these impulses, it will be difficult for you to progress. To solve this problem you will have to correct your perspective. Your perspective is sensitive to the external atmosphere. You can avoid this influence through your own thought process.

When you started your spiritual journey, your goal was self-realization but your feeling of attachment stood in the way. Psychologists use the word 'libido', which signifies sex though it is not limited to sex. Generally, psychologists use the word 'sex' to identify attachment. Until you change the flow of libido, you cannot change the direction of attachment, and you will not develop a fruitful spiritual journey. If you water a tree, it will grow. If you have more than one tree and you don't want the first tree to grow, i.e., you want another tree to grow, you will turn the flow of water pipes or sprinklers to the second tree. Otherwise you will not get the desired result. Similarly, to realize the self, you will have to change the direction of your energy.

ATTRACTION

When the energy of one person gets connected with the energy of another person, it generates an attachment or attraction. If the nature or level of the energy does not match, the people do not get attached. That is why you do not feel attracted to everyone you meet. A person who has strong energy attracts people more easily. Colour, shape and body structure do not play much of a role in the field of attraction. When favourable energies meet, they create a bond between the two people, for energy attracts energy.

Many poets have declared that a woman attracts a man through her body language and the expression of her eyes. What does this mean? I understood the secret when meditating.

Our brain produces lots of waves and energy and our eyes, fingers and speech are the points through which energy comes out of the brain. When energy released through the eyes of one person comes in contact with the energy of another person, they become infatuated and attracted. But you can change the path of energy, moving it away from attachment towards knowledge, spirituality or the soul. When this happens your libido slows down and you have fewer attachments.

Why do we want to reduce the attachment? Attachment is a conditional love for any person. It stays as long as the person is in favour. The very day the person is not in favour, the friendship turns into enmity, while the love developed through spirituality is unconditional and everlasting. Shifting the energy from attachment to spirituality brings eternal happiness.

The aim of spirituality is to destroy external attachments and create an attraction to the inner world. In spirituality, there are two types of attachments – auspicious and inauspicious. Attachment for spirituality, for our self or for another spiritual person is an auspicious attachment. One who is attached to spirituality is spiritual. So there is attachment in the spiritual world too. The only difference between the two is that the energy that was flowing to the material world now flows to the inner world. The attachment is now directed to searching for the truth.

Until you reach the state of *veetrag* (zero attachment) and your kashay is completely destroyed, you cannot stay away from attachment. But remember, this attachment or attraction is not negative. Now your attachment is empowered with spirituality. In this state, you are detached from the external world. *Anuragat veetragah*; detachment comes out of attachment. Attachment in favour of one brings detachment from another. When you develop an attraction for the self, you become detached from matter. You cannot have attachments for two opposite streams – 'soul' and 'matter' – at the same time.

People say that the instinct of sex is a natural instinct. Why should we want to change our natural instinct? Well, the answer is obvious. Sex is a natural instinct, but if we did not sublimate our natural instincts, we would be living like animals. Do you know why animals do not live like humans? It is because they do not know the process of sublimation. On the other hand, man has developed his capacities because he knows how to purify his natural instincts. He knows how to give them new value and shape. These qualities help humans stay human. If man accepts sex as a natural need and keeps enjoying it without control like an animal, civilized society as we know it will not exist. Society was formed when men made rules and enforced discipline. Animals do not know another way of living. They do not know how to utilize their energy. But man knows how to change the mode of his innate instincts.

Anger, sex and fear are innate. We are born with these instincts. You do not need to learn how to be angry but you need to learn how to forgive; you already know how to be afraid but you need to learn courage; you need not learn about sex, but you need to learn about celibacy.

Vachaspati Mishra, a great Indian writer, started writing a book. He had just got married, yet day and night he was deeply engrossed in writing his book. His energy was directed towards his writing. It took him twelve years to complete the book. Every day, for twelve years, his wife would come into his room, put oil in the lamp, and go on her way. One night, while Vachaspati was writing, his wife came in as usual to put oil in his lamp. As she was leaving the room, Vachaspati turned and asked, 'Who are you? Why are you here?'

She replied, 'I am your wife, Bhamati.'

As he heard her words, his marriage unravelled before his eyes. He told his wife, 'Please forgive me, I forgot you. I was not conscious of our marriage.'

Finally he decided to name his book *Bhamati*, after his wife. It was the greatest work he ever wrote.

Sex is a part of love or attachment. It is true that attachments are necessary for social life, but to give it unlimited freedom would be dreadful. For instance, if everyone were free to fulfil their sexual desire with anyone when they liked, then everything – family, friendships, society – would be scattered and broken.

I believe, however, that no attitude should be suppressed. Suppression can lead to depression, which is dangerous. But there should always be a limit. There are many people who do not even talk about sex. They have become scared of it, but this fear is imaginary. They pretend not to be interested in sex and sexual talk, but in fact they like it. They have sexual feelings but do not want to show them.

Sex is a fact that cannot be denied. Generally, people think it is our eyes that create sexual lust, so they think they should destroy the eyes. This is not the solution. How many eyes will you end up destroying? That will beget another problem. When you begin your spiritual practice, if you say that you stay away from sexual desires, that you have abandoned it, that you are completely detached, this is a lie. You are not only deceiving yourself, but others too. You cannot change from the first day.

Inborn instincts are aroused in any man – a spiritual practitioner as well as a common man. The practitioner is one who has started the journey of transformation. Anyone who starts this journey of transformation is a spiritual practitioner; it does not matter if he is an ascetic or an ordinary man. If you really want to change, then start the spiritual journey. Practise transmutation and spirituality, but don't show off your achievements.

WHY DOES ENERGY PROVOKE LUST?

The main reason for the flow of energy towards sex is stress. The more stressed you are, the greater your sexual desire. Stress and sexual stimulation are both a result of krishn leshya. One who is endowed with krishn leshya has no control over his sense organs. The more stress you have, the stronger your krishn leshya is. Because of stress, man gets into negative habits; he becomes passionate and commits sinful acts. And again his leshya becomes krishn by attracting karma.

I once read of a strange experiment to reduce stress. There was a lady who was overwhelmed by stress. She went to a hermitage where she was given a new treatment in which she was molested and she became relaxed. I was extremely surprised to read this. She might have relaxed on her own, for she obviously had some energy within that wanted to come out. It came out through molestation and she felt relaxed. For a fleeting moment, she might have felt good, but at the next moment what would she have felt? She would have been filled with more stress. In my perspective, this is not the right way to release the energy of stress. It can give transitory relief, but it is not a permanent solution.

There are many popular ways in society to release stress like drinking, smoking and drugs. Man takes these to free himself from stress caused by fear, worry and his surroundings.

Drinking wine to eliminate stress is not bad in itself. But it is bad when your muscles get into the habit of drinking. It is very easy to acquire the behavioural pattern of drinking until it becomes almost involuntary. Your muscles get used to it and you become addicted. This is bad for you.

Non-suppression does not mean that desires should be free and fulfilled openly. We should look for a third way, the middle way, through transformation, sublimation and purification.

Sublimation is the best way, but what are the possible techniques or steps for transformation, sublimation or purification of sexual instincts? The techniques given by spiritual science also help release stress. Moreover, these techniques are not harmful. Spirituality teaches the process of sublimation which is devoid of any negative effect.

There was a small town in which an ailment spread rapidly. Many doctors tried to find a cure but to no avail. So the king decided to seek the help of mantriks, who healed through mantras and chanting.

One mantrik said, 'I have a ghost who can cure the disease, but he is horrible to look at. If anyone mocks him, he will destroy the whole town.'

Another mantrik said, 'My ghost is also hideous but he is calm. He does not hurt anybody in any situation. He is capable of curing all diseases.'

The king told the first mantrik, 'You can go because your ghost is dangerous. He will cure the disease but he might destroy the town. We do not need such a ghost.'

Then the king turned to the second mantrik and said, 'You are assigned to cure the disease. Your ghost is good. He will cause no harm.'

My point is that there are two ways to reduce stress: by using stimulants like drugs, alcohol and tobacco or by sublimation of the attitude. The former is not a permanent solution but the latter is.

Drinking wine is an addiction. Meditation is also an addiction, but it does not have side effects. The need to release stress cannot be denied and the best way to do so is through meditation. Through meditation we get empowered. In this state, stress or any worldly addiction cannot enter our life. I will discuss the exercises to empower yourself in the next chapter.

In a nutshell, the secret of successful meditation is awareness and looking within yourself. If you have both, sexual urges will not bother you. You will not feel stressed. If you don't get stressed, you will not take drugs or alcohol to release the stress. This practice may not immediately lead you to complete detachment but your energy will definitely start flowing upward, your inner power will be awakened, your intelligence will improve, your wisdom will be revived and, finally, you will attain enlightenment.

ESSENCE

- ✤ The purpose of austerity is to open a new door and shut the old doors of natural instincts.
- ✤ There are three basic attitudes that impede inner power: anger, fear and sexual desire.
- ✤ When the energy of one person gets connected with the energy of another person, this connection causes an attraction.
- ✤ Through meditation you can redirect the energy from the material world to the inner world.

14

Aura and Awakening of Power – II

Awakening of power is imperative for developing a powerful personality.
Without awakening power, your consciousness cannot flow upward.
Consequently, you cannot attain bliss. Therefore, the first requisite is the
awakening and enrichment of power.

To empower your personality, the awakening of power is essential. It is power that helps lift the consciousness and makes you blissful.

There are two powers working within us: the power of soul and the power of taijas (bioelectricity). The power of the soul vibrates incessantly. The bioelectric body, as a microbody, is all-pervading in the physical body, helps in digestion, physical action and developing a glowing personality. Light, electricity and warmth are its attributes. The bioelectric body needs to be powerful to run a spiritual, healthy and active life. To empower this body we need to use bioelectric power from the external sources. The atoms of bioelectric power are spread throughout space. We attract them, convert them to a compatible form, and use this energy. We can only do so when the power of the soul and of our taijas sharir are fused.

Bioelectric power is a cosmic power. It is all-pervading. There is not a single point in space where bioelectric power does not exist. The only way to use this power is to awaken your inner conscious energy, the power of your soul.

The question is: How is this energy impeded and what are the obstacles in awakening this power? In the subtle body, where vibrations of conscious energy exist, there is a parallel negative energy that stops our conscious energy from rising. In Jain philosophy, this second energy is known as *antaray* or hindrance karma. Its function is to obstruct positive energy. So, even as the vibrations of conscious power seek to manifest positive energy, antaray karma actively impedes conscious energy.

So, we have to learn how to perform two simultaneous actions. The first is to remove the energy of antaray karma so that our conscious power can come out. The second is to empower bioelectric energy. This force is everywhere in the cosmos. We already have bioelectric energy within us, in the taijas sharir. To activate this energy we have to attract bioelectric atoms from the cosmos. The more atoms of bioelectric power we attract, the stronger the taijas sharir will be.

You can attract bioelectric atoms from all six directions. You need power to attract and absorb these atoms, not just physical power but also the power of the mind and of speech. All three are required to accomplish the desired effect. Do not misunderstand these as three different types of power – they are different aspects of one power.

Modern psychology generally accepts that the human mind has one power – libido, the power of sex. All other powers aim at developing the power of sex. While Freud defined libido as a sexual force, Carl Jung defined it as an energy force that drives many aspects of desire and creativity.

Spiritual philosophy also propounds that there is only one power – the power of bioelectricity, pran at the physical level. But this power is manifested in different forms to perform various actions in your life. This vital energy works as the power of speech and physical power. *Ayushya* drives your life span, *indriya* drives your sense organs, and *shvasoch-chwas* is respiratory power. Everything is one power but because of their various functions, they are given different names. To enrich this power, we need to understand its principles. Once you develop the power, you can benefit by moving it in any direction.

~

The first step to develop inner power is strengthening your determination to change the leshya, which has the strongest influence on your aura. Without changing the leshya, power can neither be developed nor used in the right way.

The key question is: How do you change your leshya? First, analyse yourself, then tell yourself: 'Certain emotions are harmful for my personality.' When you are depressed, you want to destroy your strength. You sink into passivity. Such thinking reduces the level of vital energy and degrades the personality and aura. You become like a dead soul. Now, this is where consciousness can play an important role. The first job of the consciousness is to give positive suggestions: 'I will not be a pessimist. I will never get depressed. I will make my hands and legs active. I will make use of my potential. I am optimistic, enthusiastic and I will achieve my goals.' Your mind has tremendous power. It can see the images of your thoughts.

When you create strong feelings by repeating the autosuggestions, you visualize a mental image of your autosuggestions. To give your feelings mental clarity, you will have to use your determination. Make a mental image that clarifies your goal. For example, 'I want to be this' or 'I want to do that' or 'I want to develop my powers'. Keep focusing on this image. The more you focus, the clearer the picture will become. The clearer the picture, the faster it will start taking on colour. So, first make a resolution, then develop a mental picture with constant diligence.

The second step to develop your inner power is concentration. Your complete focus should be on the image. Empty your mind of any other thought or imagination. If any thoughts come, let them go. Don't get bogged down by them. Perceive them as a mere observer. In the presence of your concentration, the power of resolution will start taking shape.

The third step is will power. Your feelings get converted into will power in the presence of positive words and inner autosuggestion. Will power is your desire. In the beginning of the process, 'to be powerful' was your goal, not your desire. But at this third stage, your goal becomes your will power, your desire.

Meditation to empower yourself:

1. Sit in meditation posture, eyes closed
2. Relax your body and practise deep breathing.
3. Bring forward a thought (goal).
4. Develop an image of the goal.
5. Focus on the image.
6. Create autosuggestions.

7. Build the will power (through autosuggestion).
8. Realize your dream or goal.
9. Open your eyes.

When your resolution, concentration and will power come together, your leshya begins to transform. When the leshya changes, the aura changes.

Sometimes you are sitting quietly and you suddenly conjure up undesired thoughts. Your thoughts keep changing. Why do you get such thoughts? Where do these thoughts come from?

The atoms of thoughts are everywhere, and constantly on the move. The thoughts of millions of people are there in the cosmos. When you fall under the range of these thoughts, the same thoughts are created in your mind. Don't believe that your thoughts are unique. They can belong to someone else or to several other people. It is very hard to decide which thoughts belong to you and which belong to others.

This world of thoughts is all-pervasive; no person can exist beyond this sphere. If you are in a forest and there is no other soul, not even a bird, you are still not alone. The subtle atoms of the universe constantly move around you and these unseen thoughts influence you. It is interesting that these thoughts do not look for an empty, clear mind. They are guided to people who are full of thoughts.

The question is: Can you stop these incoming thoughts? Until you make your aura powerful, you cannot stop the barrage of these unseen thoughts. When your leshya becomes tejo and your aura becomes red, the doors are closed. In this state not a single thought can enter. The same thing occurs when your aura is yellow. And when your aura is white, all thoughts stop. In this state you are thoughtless. All external influences are blocked. This is the moment that you are alone. In spite of living in society, you are aware of your own self.

When your physical aura and psychical aura are powerful, all external energies are stopped from entering your body. To awaken your power, you have to remain alert and vigilant. This cannot happen without awareness. You must develop an awareness of your inner world, because it is your inner conscious vibrations that give shape and colour to the physical aura, leshya and conscious aura.

I have talked about three steps – the power of determination, the power of concentration and the power of the will. These are the steps to enhance the power or energy. Yet, this is not the complete process. The complete process includes saving energy by stopping the misuse of the energy.

More power is consumed when it goes to the sense organs – sex, touch, taste, smell and other sensory objects. A great deal of energy is drained out in the use of these organs. You need not make an effort to direct the flow of your energy towards your sense organs; energy goes there by default. Whenever you feel an urge – of sex, possessiveness, anger, deceit, or food – and you carry out the action accordingly, you are depleting your energy. So, if you want to save the energy, minimize these activities.

The following meditation exercises help to save the energy.

1. Relaxation or body meditation
2. Silence or vocal meditation
3. No-thought state or mental meditation
4. Experiencing the inner subtle vibrations

These are four independent exercises. You can perform any one at a time.

1. RELAXATION OR BODY MEDITATION

In the first exercise, kayotsarg, you relax your body completely, until your body is still and your mind is focused on each part of the body, telling them to relax. Experience the relaxation of every cell in your body. They can retain their energy. Thereafter, stay calm and slow down your breathing. Take long breaths. When your breathing is slow, you feel relaxed. Moreover, through kayotsarg you get control over your body. Your body requires less oxygen. The use of vital energy is reduced in this state and you save energy.

2. SILENCE OR VOCAL MEDITATION

The second practice is vocal meditation. To save your energy, take care of yourself. Speak less, and do not speak unnecessarily. While speaking your vocal cords have to work a lot and a great deal of energy is drained. Try to remain silent; you will save energy. Furthermore, you can use this energy later. Thus, to save your energy, control your speech and be silent.

3. NO-THOUGHT STATE OR MENTAL MEDITATION

In the third exercise, try not to think, as thoughts bring about stress. Learn to break the chain of thoughts and focus on your breathing. Eventually there will be no thoughts. You will just experience the inner self. A no-thought state assists in the elimination of stress. The chain of thoughts uses a lot of energy which is difficult to replenish. The only solution is to try to stay in a no-thought state.

It will reduce the use of energy, and save more energy. This will help you manage stress.

4. EXPERIENCING THE INNER SUBTLE VIBRATIONS

The fourth exercise is experiencing the inner subtle vibrations, which is a significant step in the alleviation of stress. When you experience the vibrations of a material object, you feel stressed. On the other hand, when you start feeling inner vibrations, the vibrations of bliss are awakened and you feel divine happiness. Until you awaken these vibrations you will not find a new way. Until you experience the vibrations of bright red energy you cannot feel any change. Red brings spirituality. In the state of tejo leshya the energy of attachment changes its flow. This is the process of sublimation.

Do not expect to get results in one day. Keep practising, and one day you will reach your destination. Until then you have to analyse where you have reached every day and record your progress. How far have you come? Are you moving ahead or back?

In short, you can retain energy in two ways:

1. Through various exercises of vital energy and breathing exercises.
2. By not wasting your energy.

To empower yourself, save your vital energy by cutting down on sensual pleasure.

Many people have asked me: Does samadhi or peace begin with sensual pleasure? Many people think that use of the senses – watching favorite scenes, hearing, eating, touching and other physical activities give satisfaction and happiness. Nowadays it is emphasized that you should do what makes you happy. But that is not the right way to find peace and happiness. You want to develop your power, but you cannot develop it until you stop its diversions. If you are trying to improve your power and it is being depleted at the same time, how can you achieve your goal? If a river keeps flowing, energy cannot be produced in one location. But after building a dam to stop the flow of water, the resultant regulated water can be used to produce electric power. Therefore, we need to control the incessant flow of innate instincts to save our energy. To stop the constant consumption of energy it is necessary to consolidate our energy.

Peace through sensual or physical pleasure – such a thought builds confusion in society. Some people believe that sexual pleasure is a great way to attain peace. Whatever may be the intention behind introducing this concept, the fact is that the common public cannot understand this secret. The practice of tantra was introduced primarily with spiritual practices that aim at liberation from ignorance and rebirth. The tantric practitioner seeks to use the pran that flows through the universe, including one's own body, to attain purposeful goals. These goals may be spiritual, material or both. Tantrism is a quest for spiritual perfection and magical power, which can be powerful enough to bring the desired result. To avoid the misuse of this power the study and practice of tantra was kept secret and had limited access. Unfortunately, when the practice of tantra was disclosed to common people, it was misused and even identified as black magic. For many modern readers in the west, 'Tantra' has become a synonym for 'spiritual sex' or 'sacred sexuality', a belief that sex ought to be recognized as a sacred act that is capable of elevating its participants to a more sublime spiritual plane. So, if one does not understand the secret and purpose, an ordinary man can lose his way. The tantric belief is in favour of sexual enjoyment, which creates a state of no-thought and makes a person feel happy. This state of no-thought and pleasure gives peace. Man searched for peace because he felt pleasure in the state of no-thought.

To use another example: When a hunter fixes his target, he becomes so immersed in his task that he has no thought of time. His concentration is at its peak. The hunter achieves peace at this moment. Similarly, a robber is focused on robbing. Then why don't we accept that this is also a source of peace? Lord Mahavir also considered such activities meditation. The only condition of meditation is concentration. Remember, meditation can be both positive and negative. Concentration on an unsocial or worldly act is inauspicious meditation.

There was a great archer. He was proud of his skill. Once, he met a man who told him that his guru was an expert at targeting the victim without the help of a bow and arrow. The archer was very surprised. He became curious to meet his guru, so he went with him. The guru took them to the top of a hill and stood on a rock. Below the rock was a deep pit.

The guru focused on the sky. A group of birds were flying overhead. As soon as the birds came within range of his eyes, they began to fall, one by one, into the pit. This is how the guru targetted the birds. Is this not meditation? Of course, it needs a lot of concentration. But all techniques of concentration are not meditation or samadhi. We cannot say that the concentration needed in robbery, hunting, sex or other such acts are real meditation.

Some people think that sexual enjoyment is the way to meditation. If sexual enjoyment gives peace, why does one need to attend meditation camps? Why should one meditate? If meditation happens naturally, why should one make the effort? Do not get confused by the term 'meditation'. The same word is used in different contexts. Worldly acts and the spiritual journey can both be called meditation. Do not get stuck on a name. Try to understand the reality of what the name represents. While it can be accepted that sexual desire might have inspired some to search for a pleasure beyond that of sex, sexual pleasure alone can never be accepted as true meditation.

～

The science of logic explains a process of evaluating the root. If a man knows about stone, he then wants to know the mine from which the stone was sourced. If he can know one man, he can know all living beings. If you know the source, you know the complete reality. We should understand the need for meditation in the same way.

The practice of meditation was adopted by ancient ascetics in their search for bliss and eternal happiness. But how did they figure out that meditation could bring them everlasting happiness? There was a chain of logical thoughts in their own experiences. They found that man feels happy when he eats the food he likes. He enjoys playing, listening to music, dancing, talking, travelling and other worldly activities. Everything gives a certain degree of pleasure. But this pleasure is not permanent. After satisfying one desire you seek something else to find happiness. Moreover, physical pleasure weakens your power, creates toxins in your body and affects your thoughts. This disappointment with temporary happiness from material pleasure encouraged the ancient ascetics to search for eternal happiness.

Lord Mahavir has said: '*Khanmetta-sokkha, bahukal dukkha.*' All sensual objects give momentary happiness, but their end is painful.

The period of action and result can be defined in two ways:

1. In the period of action the object gives pleasure but the final result is painful for ever.
2. In the period of action the object gives pain but finally it gives happiness for ever.

For example, when you eat sweets, you feel good while you are eating them, but in the end it can lead to diabetes and other illnesses. It gives immediate pleasure but the result is harmful. If you eat amla it might taste bitter and sour, but it is good for your health. Here, you may not like the immediate sensations but the result is positive. You should judge the quality of an action by the result. The process of meditation was also discovered on the basis of results. When you focus on the action in terms of instant gratification, you enable the loss of energy. Your energy is drained, and you do not achieve anything. Man wanted a good activity with good results; he wanted happiness both during the action and in the outcome. This led him to meditation, a way to save energy and make the aura bright.

The founders of occult science proposed two types of auras:

1. Emotional aura
2. Mental aura

We believe in the same concepts in the theory of leshya. There are two types of leshya:

1. Kashay leshya: *Kashay-pravritti-ranjita leshya* – an aural colouration (leshya) influenced by arousal of passion. Kashay leshya creates an emotional aura. If anger (a form of kashay) is active, the colour and quality of the emotional aura will correspond with this emotion.
2. Yog leshya: Yog leshya is formed by the activity of body, mind and vocal cords. Yog leshya creates a mental aura.

The stronger the force of kashay, the more your energy is drained, which in turn weakens the bioelectric body. If the body, mind and speech are more active, you are using more energy and thereby depleting it. This means that you cannot accumulate it. Without storing energy, you cannot open the new dimensions of austerity in your life. Therefore, you need to stop the unnecessary use of energy.

You can enrich the treasure of power when you attract power through the practice of determination, through accumulating vital energy, through inhaling your energy and by controlling the use of energy. Consequently, you will be able to generate a strong aura around you, which will protect you from external evils and negative energy.

ESSENCE

- ✤ Everybody wants to enhance their power. There are two sources of power – soul and bioelectric power.
- ✤ The atoms of bioelectric power are ubiquitous and ever present. You can attract them to enhance your power.
- ✤ Leshya of spirituality allows energy to flow towards the psychical state of 'know the self, realize the self'.
- ✤ Leshya of non-spirituality pushes energy to flow towards the mental state of controlling, ruling and cheating others.
- ✤ Lord Mahavir said, 'All sensual objects give momentary happiness, but their end is painful.'
- ✤ A powerful aura restricts foreign elements from entering the body, mind and soul.
- ✤ There are two types of aura – mental aura and emotional aura.

15
Leshya: A Technique of Healing

Spiritual healing keeps your emotions healthy and meditation is the tool.
The purpose of meditation is to purify emotions and thoughts and maintain
physical, mental and emotional health.

We are living in a world where, from sunrise to sunset, we see contradictions. Not a single man or object lives without contradiction. There is no one who is completely healthy, and at the same time there is no one who is completely sick. A wise man has some foolishness in him, and a mad man will have a bit of wisdom. This is the law of the universe. We cannot change it; all we can do is have a balanced perspective. We do not have control over the contradictions, but we can create harmony.

There are as many solutions as there are problems. The body gets sick, therefore sickness is a problem. So man developed a healing technique as a solution to the sickness. Similarly, negative emotions are a problem. Spiritual healing is a technique to make the emotions healthy and positive, and the tool for spiritual healing is meditation. The purpose of meditation is to purify emotions and thoughts, and also maintain physical, mental and emotional health.

We practise long breathing to discard the toxins stored within. The purpose of throwing out toxins is to allow pure vital energy to enter the body. Alternate breathing (*samavritti shvas preksha*) is practised to break delusion and to enhance awareness of the mind. Delusion and awareness are two opposite streams. One who wants to awaken the self is a supporter of vigilance or awareness. The supporters of delusion stay away from spirituality. They coax people into the consumption of intoxicants like alcohol, tobacco, cocaine and opium, which make you feel euphoric or altered, and take you away from your soul and rational thought. Thus the stream of delusion hides self-awareness.

Preksha meditation is not a stream of delusion; it is the way to awareness. The objective of preksha meditation is constant awareness, not to overlook the self even for a moment, and to experience the existence of the self incessantly. Meditation in which man loses his self-awareness and becomes unconscious is not real meditation. Peace achieved at the cost of self-existence is not the state of awakening.

Long breathing (*dirgh shvas preksha*) helps you rupture this delusion. It gives you mental peace and stability. It does not let you become unaware or lax in the cognizance of the experience. In the practice of long breathing, you try to stay conscious. In the exercise of *samavritti shvas preksha* or *anulom-vilom pranayam* too, your mind needs to remain alert. A break in awareness of the mind, even for a moment, fractures the rhythm.

In anulom-vilom or alternate breathing, you inhale through the left nostril, then exhale through the right. Next, inhale through the right nostril and exhale through the left. This is one cycle. Repeat this cycle at least 9 times.

Similarly, perception of the body requires focus, otherwise you may unwittingly fall asleep. You can perceive every part of your body only if you are completely aware and beyond thoughts. You must be removed from emotions like attachment and hate while perceiving your body. The practice of perceiving the psychical centre and the practice of purifying emotion are also practices of awareness. If your emotions are not pure, your thoughts will not be pure. We need to purify both.

In our subtle body, two types of vibrations move in parallel ways – the vibrations of attachment and the vibrations of detachment. These vibrations eventually get converted to emotions. Kashay and attachment are correlated. As kashay reduces, attachment grows weaker. However, the instinct of attachment does not get destroyed; it simply becomes inert. When the vibrations of detachment get stronger, tejo, padm and shukla leshya and the corresponding emotions become more powerful. However, if the vibrations of attachment are strongly active, vibrations of neel and kapot become powerful while tejo and padm leshya get diminished.

So there are two contradictory groups: one with three dark leshya and the other with three light leshya. Lord Mahavir said, 'Three leshya are auspicious and three leshya are inauspicious. Three leshya are dry and three are smooth. Three are cold and three are hot.' This is a very important statement for understanding emotions.

A similar concept is found in colour-science, where colour is divided in two – light colours and dark colours. One is hot and the other is cold. Hot colours have a warm effect while the cold ones have a calming effect. Four shadows of colour are explained: 1) Hot colour and light tint, 2) Hot colour and dark tint, 3) Cold colour and light tint, and 4) Cold colour and dark tint.

According to Jain philosophy, black, blue and grey correspond with the leshya that are cold and dry. When these leshya become active and subsequent vibrations are awakened, they result in emotions like jealousy, sadness, hatred and fear. Therefore, negative emotions are caused by dark colours.

Tejo, padm and shukla leshya are hot and smooth. When the vibrations of these leshya become active, the metamorphosis of the emotions begins. Such vibrations lead to emotions like courage, friendliness, peace, self-control and forgiveness. If the emotions are pure, thoughts will follow.

~

While thoughts have no immediate connection with kashay, as they are linked to our brain, our emotions are concerned with the endocrine glands. There are two agencies for expressing emotions in the body – the endocrine system and the nervous system. The endocrine system expresses our emotions and the nervous system produces thoughts.

Thoughts are not the precursor of emotions. Emotions are part of the internal system while thoughts are part of the execution system. Emotions follow the leshya and thoughts follow emotion. The catalyst for the entire process is emotion; therefore you do not need to focus on your thoughts. To make yourself positive you need not work on deleting negative thoughts. Purify your emotions instead. If you do this, your thoughts will become pure by default.

COLOUR MEDITATION

The simplest way to purify emotions is through colour meditation. This is a highly significant technique. Meditating on smooth colours helps to purify emotions. Yellow, red and white are the three colours that can purify emotions.

Tantric practice also has some techniques of colour meditation:

1. The meditator tries to perceive the red colour of the rising sun on his whole body. This meditation can lead him to the state of veetrag (complete detachment).
2. The meditator tries to imagine that his body is in the sky and then visualizes the colour of the sunset in winter. Six months of this practice brings the meditator to the highest point of veetrag.
3. By focusing on the tip of the nose along with golden or white colour, one can get rid of negative thoughts.

Several experiments can be found in Tantra for developing higher consciousness, self-control, knowledge and veetrag. All these experiments are parallel to the principal of leshya.

Colours are very significant. Colours dominate the entire emotional system. Colours can cure physical ailments and mental weakness and develop spiritual awareness.

To cure psychological problems, visualize the colour of the rising sun at darshan kendra. Rising-sun meditation activates the energy of tejo leshya. This energy helps heal mental weakness and problems.

When somebody has a negative emotion, eventually the emotion falls by the wayside, leaving behind the toxins of thought. These toxins bother and inflict pain in terms of physical or mental problems. Finally, the person becomes stressed and unbalanced. If you visualize the word *arham* in bright white colour, it helps cure many physical ailments by cleansing your body of toxins.

Through meditation of arham, emotions are also altered, surprisingly. When you focus on warm colours (yellow, red and white) and go into deep meditation, your emotions change. You need not worry about the transformation, for it happens naturally. All your negative vibrations get transformed. The vibrations of warm colours prevent the vibrations of attachments from rising, making them powerless. At the same time, the vibrations of detachment become active. Red and orange make the body alert and each cell of the body gets energized.

Colour meditation helps strengthen the body and mind. It improves memory and intelligence. It purifies the aura and emotions.

MANTRA

The second powerful tool to transform emotion is words. Mantra, a special combination of words, can transform emotions. Once a person sets an emotion in place, it gets rooted in his nature. It is hard to modify or remove that emotion. Only an intelligent person will be successful in transforming emotions once it is set. Each letter has its own vibration and energy. The special combination of the letters in a mantra makes the word more powerful. When we chant the mantra the vibrations are produced inside the body and these vibrations change the frequency of our emotions. Therefore, a mantra has great healing power.

A man called a doctor and complained that he was very sick and feeling extremely nervous. The doctor looked at his face, and understood his nervousness right away. The doctor said, 'Don't worry. You will be fine by evening. You will start walking and moving. Your nervousness will be gone. My medicine will cure you very fast.' He went outside. He made a packet of a mixture of ashes and salt and came back. Giving the packet to the patient, he said, 'It is a very powerful medicine. Only two doses will cure you.'

The patient took the two doses and started feeling better. The next evening when he went to the doctor, he no longer felt ill. Was it the magic of the medicine? No, the medicine was merely a placebo. The real magic was in the words of the doctor, which penetrated the patient at the emotional level.

Let me tell you another story. Acharya Bhikshu, before he became a monk, once went travelling on a camel, accompanied by a friend. His friend was addicted to tobacco, and halfway through the journey, he ran out. It became difficult for him to continue. His body went through withdrawal symptoms and he started feeling weak. He stopped walking and sat down.

Acharya Bhikshu asked him, 'What happened? Why are you so lethargic?'

His friend replied, 'I can't move. I finished all my tobacco and I need more. Until I get some tobacco it is impossible for me to continue.'

The Acharya said, 'Okay, don't worry, I will try to get some more from a passerby.' He went in search of people, but could not find anybody. He then took dry cow dung, powdered it and went back to his friend. He told his friend, 'I found a traveller who had some tobacco. It is not very good, but it'll work for the time being.'

His friend opened the packet, smelled it, and replied, 'Let's go now. It is more than enough for me to reach home.'

How did this happen? The cow dung obviously didn't turn into tobacco. It was his words that convinced his friend. Words have infinite power to change emotions. If the words of one person can reach the emotions of another, they can change everything.

In another instance, a woman's daughter-in-law was very aggressive, and everybody in the family was tired of her nature. The mother-in-law took her to the doctor.

The girl told him, 'I am very aggressive and ill-tempered. Can you prescribe me something that can help calm my fits of rage?'

Giving her a syrup, the doctor told her, 'Whenever you start feeling angry, take this syrup, swirl it in your mouth for several minutes, and then swallow it. This is a very effective medicine.'

In ten days the girl's anger cooled and she was no longer moody. The medicine that the doctor had provided was actually plain water. Yet, it worked better than a medicine because of the suggestion of his words.

George Ivanovich Gurdjieff was a great Russian spiritual leader. One day his father told him, 'Whenever you start feeling angry, don't express your anger for twenty-four hours. You can get angry after twenty-four hours.' This advice became the treasure of his life and led him to become a great spiritual practitioner. Can anybody express anger twenty-four hours after they felt angry? Never. The anger vanishes. Whenever the heat of energy becomes active, if you make use of it right away, you will get angry; if you don't, the heat subsides.

Words are strong instruments in transforming emotions. When you take words to the emotional level, you get the expected result. You should select and use the right words and choose powerful instructions so that your words can penetrate at the emotional level. Your words should beat the vibrations of attachment. If this happens, the transformation has begun. Selecting the correct words is an important task. It is hard to change a person, but the force of perfect words can do this. If you utilize the power of words and select the perfect words, you can bring a great change not only in your emotional state but also in that of others.

I have composed nine phrases of *mangal bhavna* (auspicious thinking). Reciting these every day with awareness will help you transform your emotions and heal you.

1. *Shree sampanno-ham shyaam*
   Let me be endowed with (spiritual) wealth.
2. *Hree sampanno-ham shyaam*
   Let me be endowed with self-discipline.
3. *Dhee sampanno-ham shyaam*
   Let me be endowed with intelligence.
4. *Dhriti sampanno-ham shyaam*
   Let me be endowed with patience.
5. *Shakti sampanno-ham shyaam*
   Let me be endowed with strength.
6. *Shanti sampanno-ham shyaam*
   Let me be endowed with peace.
7. *Nandi sampanno-ham shyaam*
   Let me be endowed with bliss.

8. *Tejah sampanno-ham shyaam*
   Let me be endowed with magnificence.
9. *Shuklah sampanno-ham shyaam*
   Let me be endowed with purity.

Through colour meditation and mantra chanting you can heal your body, mind and soul. If you do so, the concept of leshya will become more of a healing therapy than a philosophy.

ESSENCE

- ❖ Our life is full of contradictions like pain and pleasure, life and death, and so on. We do not have control over these contradictions, but we can create harmony.
- ❖ There are two main facets of life: emotions and thoughts.
- ❖ Emotions and thoughts biased by kashay hassle and provoke man, whereas emotions and thoughts rooted in knowledge lead to pure consciousness.
- ❖ Spiritual health means the end of delusion.
- ❖ Mental health means the end of mental weakness.
- ❖ Physical health means the end of toxins produced by polluted thoughts.
- ❖ Colour meditation and mantra chanting can bring about a positive change to emotions.
- ❖ Long breathing helps to rupture delusion.
- ❖ Words are strong instruments in transforming emotions. When you take perfect words to the emotional level, you get the expected results.

16

Leshya: A Technique of Altering Your Bio-chemistry

Spirituality is actually a science of chemicals, a process to change chemicals. Through meditation you can produce chemicals that make the chemicals of kashay ineffective. You can disintegrate their strength, lessen their impact, even cease their encroachment. These new chemicals give you a new experience.

Toxins and nectar are both chemicals. Ayurveda has done extensive research on chemicals. The great Ayurvedic scholars used chemicals in ways that kept people healthy by removing all toxins. Spirituality is actually a science of chemicals, a process to change the chemicals. A student of chemistry knows that by altering the quality of chemicals of an object one can change the object. The same principle works on human chemistry. One who has worked on human alchemy and knows the chemical structures of the human body knows that the flux of chemicals in our bodies can bring about a change in us. The techniques of meditation, yoga and fasting are all techniques of chemical transformation.

FASTING

Lord Mahavir was asked, 'Lord! What should be done to develop celibacy?'

Lord Mahavir replied, *'Avi nib-balaa-saye'*. Eat light food.

Don't consume powerful food. Don't take spicy and heavy food. Take food that can satisfy your biological hunger. Don't take food that provokes lust.

The disciple asked again, 'Lord! What more should be done?'

Lord Mahavir replied, 'Eat less, so that you will not have enough chemicals to stimulate lust.'

There are several causes for the stimulation of the sexual instinct. One of them is excess fat and blood in the body. It means obese people are more likely to have the urge for lust because the chemicals in their bodies are powerful enough to intensify sexual desire. The quality of the instinct depends upon the quality of the chemicals inside the body.

Lord Mahavir was asked again, 'Lord! What should be done next?'

He replied, 'If you feel that it is hard to control your sexual desire then give up food.

When you leave food and practice fasting for a long time, for about ten or twenty days, your sense organs do not get the chemicals from food and they become silent. When you do not eat, the senses cool down. While fasting, a person becomes quiet. This is because the chemicals in the body are modified when you fast. Old chemicals are changed, the sense organs slow down and the sexual instinct subsides. New chemicals do not stimulate these instincts. When the sense organs are quiet, the mind and body are quiet. Fasting also has healing properties, for the chemicals produced by fasting can cure physical illnesses.

Today, people are not very familiar with this aspect of fasting. Aesculapius of ancient Greece once said, 'Instead of using medicine, fast.' In the western world, much research is being done, many experiments have been performed and the technique of fasting is slowly being introduced as a healing technique. A. J. Carlson, Professor of Physiology at the University of Chicago, states that a healthy, well-nourished man can live about 50-75 days without food, provided he is not exposed to harsh elements or emotional stress.

Dr Ray Walford, a famous UCLA researcher, said, 'Undernutrition is thus far the only method we know of that consistently retards the ageing process and extends the maximum life span of warm-blooded animals. These studies are undoubtedly applicable to humans because it works in every species studied so far.'

The studies have also concluded that restricting food to the body will improve the immune system and slow down the body's physiological deterioration. Fasting is principally a method of giving the digestive system a day off so that the process of healing can take place. This technique is used to cure diseases because of the intrinsic chemical changes that occur during fasting.

There are many forms of fasting. For example, *ayambil* is a type of fasting in which only one type of grain is taken with water once a day. There are many other forms such as alternate fasting, one-day fasts, five-day fasts, eight-day fasts, eating less, eating fewer items – all these change the bio-chemistry of the body.

Fasting is a healing process only if it is done with proper guidance and in the correct fashion. Before starting the fast one must know how and what to eat before and after fasting, and one should fast only as long as the body permits.

PRAYASCHITTA

There is no doubt that fasting, self-control and yogic exercise can bring about chemical changes. There is one more process called *prayaschitta* or atonement, which also changes the chemicals. Prayaschitta is atonement for a sin or a mistake through introspection. It is an ancient method, now called 'self-analysis' by modern psychologists.

This process involves four steps:

1) Introspection: thinking of your mistake
2) Confession: admitting to your mistake
3) Repentance: asking for forgiveness
4) Penalty: punishment in terms of spiritual exercise, positive attitude or resolution

For example, Raj dislikes his colleague and does not behave properly with him. He is stressed the whole day. In this mental state his bio-chemicals change and become negative. He is heavy-hearted and carries the negativity with him all the time. One day he analyses himself and thinks that he can control his emotions and stay calm. He realizes his mistakes and repents for his misbehaviour. After this, he feels light and free from all stress. This repentance changes his bio-chemicals and he starts building a good relationship with his colleague. This is the process of prayaschitta. When one gets the pure feeling of prayaschitta, the old humps of negativity disappear.

VINAY

Vinay (reverence) ia another important tool for changing your bio-chemistry. There is some confusion regarding reverence.

People think it means being humble towards others, but this is not a complete explanation. Misconception of the meaning of reverence has led to people believing that younger people must respect elders, and that older or senior people do not need to be modest or respectful to their juniors. This is an illusion. Reverence is necessary for the self.

Reverence means an absence of arrogance. It is a state of consciousness. We must understand that reverence forms a parts of our nature, and venerate it as such. By believing that reverence is expressed for others, we stay rigid in our egos, expecting respect from others in return. The highest spirituality is to be polite and free from ego.

There are seven types of reverence:

1. Respect for knowledge
2. Respect for faith
3. Respect for conduct
4. Modesty of mind
5. Modesty of speech
6. Modesty of body
7. Observance of formal etiquette (towards elders).

To fold hands or shake hands when greeting another is a sign of formal respect. But actual reverence means to train the mind to be modest. Keeping your mind away from ego is mental reverence.

Speaking softly and respectfully is verbal reverence.

Humility in your body language is physical reverence.

Having firm conviction and devotion for knowledge is reverence to knowledge.

Keeping your perspective straightforward, clear and relative is reverence for faith.

Doing pure and good deeds is to conduct oneself with humility.

These are all aspects of reverence or humility, which is necessary for both young and old. On the other hand, formal respect is done for the gratification of others. These formalities are followed by everybody, merely forms of social courtesy. I do not say that etiquette should be ignored but at the same time, we must develop true reverence. By following and practising true reverence you begin to change your bio-chemistry.

SWADHYAY

Another effective process of chemical change is *swadhyay* (scriptural study). When you read good literature repeatedly, your mind gets customized to new positive thoughts. The positive thoughts bring a permanent change in your chemicals.

MEDITATION

Meditation is the most powerful tool for bringing bio-chemical changes. You can produce chemicals through meditation that make the chemicals of kashay ineffective. You can disintegrate their strength, lessen their impact, even cease their encroachment. These new chemicals give you a new experience. Meditation can be practiced in various ways like colour meditation, sharir preksha, contemplation and perception of psychic centres etc.

While practising perception of psychic centres, we focus on each centre one by one. Stay there for a while and experience the subtle vibrations. Deep concentration awakens the psychic centres. When you meditate on psychic centres, you cleanse the impurities inside them. When the impurities are cleansed, you start realizing the purity of the soul. It is only when your psychic centres are uncontaminated that the conscious rays come out at the experiential level.

Before this cleansing, you have knowledge, you enjoy happiness but you do not experience reality. The subject of your knowledge is the external world. Your knowledge is acquired through your brain and induced by your nervous system. You are not familiar with the wisdom that is connected to your inner world. You have experienced pleasure, but it is pleasure that comes from the material world. You still have to experience the inner happiness where matter is irrelevant.

You are not familiar with your inner knowledge and consciousness. You are not truly aware of spiritual happiness, and you cannot attain inner knowledge, inner joy and inner bliss unless you transform your leshya by meditating on the psychic centres and you transform your emotional systems by changing the colour, smell, taste and touch of these emotions. Though each leshya has its own colour, smell, touch and taste, you are not aware of it because you are so deeply engrossed in the material world that separates you from your true reality.

Once, a powerful saint visited a city. The king heard about him, and wanted to meet him. He felt very peaceful in the presence of the saint and invited him to come and stay at the palace.

The saint replied, 'I get the smell of gold in the palace. I cannot stay there.'

'What are you talking about?' the king asked in surprise. 'What is the smell of gold? People run after gold. I have been living there for so long and yet I do not get the smell of gold.'

The saint asked the king to go with him to a colony of cobblers. As soon as the king entered the colony, he covered his nose because of the smell. The saint stopped at the house of a cobbler.

The king asked, 'Where have you brought me? The stench of leather is bothering me. I am feeling suffocated. Please let us go.'

The saint replied, 'What smell are you talking about? Why don't you ask the owner of this house?'

Meanwhile, the owner came out, and the saint asked him, 'Do you smell any stench?'

'I have been living here for many years. I have never noticed any stench,' the cobbler replied.

The saint returned with the king to the palace. He said, 'You smelt leather in that colony. But the people residing there did not smell it. In the same way, here in the palace, I detect the stench of gold, but you don't. A person accepts the milieu of the environment in which he lives.'

Man is so immersed in the smell, taste and touch of evil emotions that he does not realize that they are bad. He feels connected to them.

THE NATURE OF THE LESHYAS

Krishn leshya is black. It has a stench that is worse than that of a dead dog. This unpleasant smell is situated deep within you. Sometimes you wear perfume to hide a bad smell, but that only masks the external smell. You still carry the internal stench. The taste of krishn leshya is far more bitter than the taste of neem; its touch is infinitely harsher than the touch of a cow's tongue. You carry atoms of krishn leshya in your aura. Your aura is a constant presence in your life. Consequently, an aura characterized by krishn leshya will pervade every moment of your existence.

Similarly, you carry the aura of neel leshya and kapot leshya. The taste of the atoms of neel leshya is more pungent than the taste of trikatu (a mixture of dry ginger, long pepper and black pepper) and the gajpipal herb.The taste of kapot leshya is more astringent than an unripe mango.

Dr Josephine C. Trust was a scientist gifted with the ability to see the light and aura of people and spirits. She believed that people who are cruel have an impure and dull aura around them, while pure-hearted people have a bright, shining and lucid aura. Various colours of the aura are interpreted as representing different attitudes – golden yellow represents spiritualism, light blue represents curative ability, pink represents love and affection.

Semyon Davidovich Kirlian was a Russian inventor and researcher who, with his wife Valentina Khrisanovna Kirlian, discovered Kirlian photography in 1939. Kirlian photography allegedly depicts the body's aura. During the procedure, the object is placed on a photographic emulsion within an apparatus. The resulting photo shows a fuzzy glow surrounding the outline of the object. Kirlian photography is alleged to detect diseases (even before the physical signs appear) and emotional states. Later, based on Kirlian photography, Konstantin Korotkov, deputy director of the St Petersburg Research Institute, developed the gas-discharge visualization (GDV) technique which is widely used to measure stress and monitor the progress of medical treatments.

We do not pay as much attention to our aura and emotions as we pay to cleaning our body and clothes. Consequently, we look healthy and smart on the outside but our internal impurities wreak havoc on our mind. The mind becomes fragile. In such a situation, how can anyone be at peace? We say the world is full of turmoil. If the chemicals residing in you are turbulent for your mind, how can you expect the world to be peaceful?

Your character can be determined through your sweat. If you are aggressive, jealous, contentious and have a polluted mind, your sweat will have a kind of unpleasant smell. If you are straightforward and not hypocritical your sweat will have a pleasant smell. The Jain tradition believes that the fragrance of a lotus comes from the bodies of the Jain prophets. This scent is the symbol of auspicious emotions. If you are pure, lucid and simple, your body and mind will be pure and it will give a pleasant smell.

Denise Chen, a psychologist at Rice University, conducted research that provided direct behavioural evidence that human sweat contains emotional meanings. Sweat contains minerals like sodium, potassium, calcium, magnesium etc. The deficiency or imbalance of minerals affects the mood and emotions of a person. Moreover, the function of sweat glands is related to the nervous system. The body produces some bacteria in the presence of sweat. An individual's body odour is also influenced by diet, lifestyle, gender, genetics, health and medication.

The colour, smell, taste and touch of tejo, padm and shukla leshya are auspicious. The colour of tejo leshya is red, like the rising sun. Padm leshya is yellow, like turmeric. The colour of shukla leshya is white, like a conch shell. The smell of these three leshya is stronger than the fragrance of flowers. They taste sweeter than dates and raisins. They feel softer than butter.

A spiritual practitioner brings about bio-chemical changes through fasting and meditation. Colour meditation brings about the same effect. Once you understand the technique for transforming leshya, you will start transforming the chemicals.

EXTERNAL AND INTERNAL TOOLS FOR TRANSFORMING THE CHEMICALS

There are two tools for transforming chemicals: *tap* and matter. Tap or penance involves fasting, studying spiritual books and meditation. Matter refers to material objects like drugs, medicines or injections. The medical research referred to here doesn't necessarily come from modern research. In ancient times, many spiritual practitioners discovered medicines that could bring amazing changes in the bio-chemicals. If you felt fear, they would give you some medicine to overcome it. If a man talked while sleeping or had horrible dreams, they would put a herb near his head while he was asleep and the dreams would stop. If someone was strongly stimulated by sexual desire, they had herbs to diminish his lust. I have studied Ayurveda literature deeply, and have realized that there is a herb that can help us control our senses.

Therefore the saying goes: '*Achintya mani-mantra-aushasdhinam prabhavah*'. The effect of gems, mantras and herbal medicine is indubitable. One cannot even imagine its effects.

Your ultimate aim should be the upward flow of energy, because this is the key to opening the door of inner knowledge and self-realization. For this, mere chemical alteration is not sufficient. Chemicals might be able to control anger, sexual desire or other instincts but inner knowledge and bliss cannot be attained through external chemicals. You need a positive approach. This positive approach is the process of strengthening the mind, purifying your emotions through penance and meditation, and awakening the psychic centre.

> The effects of awakening the psychic centre:
> - It alters the chemicals, controls anger and other negative emotions, and ends all addictions and bad habits.
> - Rays of purity emerging from the psychic centre unlock the door of inner bliss and knowledge.

These two effects are explained by Lord Mahavir. Without purification of leshya, realization of your previous life (*jati-smriti gyan*), clairvoyant knowledge, mind-reading knowledge and finally *keval* or omniscience cannot be attained. Pure or crystallized knowledge is possible only through purifying the leshya. When the leshya gets changed from inauspicious to auspicious, your inner power is awakened and this power or energy alters the chemicals, and finally reveals hidden knowledge and bliss.

You should practise mangal bhavna (auspicious thinking) and meditation which will lead to simplicity, contentment and peace outwardly and awaken pure knowledge internally. By awakening the psychic centres you can stop negative effects and bring about positive effects.

Your goal is to bring about a change at both levels – outer and inner. With external chemical changes, delusion is broken and inner consciousness is uncovered; this is the state you really want to attain.

ESSENCE

❖ You have accumulated harmful chemicals inside your body. Yet, you try to stay neat and clean externally.

❖ You need to focus on the purity of the inner world.

❖ Bring about chemical changes by awakening the inner bliss and reducing the effect of karma.

❖ You can bring about bio-chemical changes:
- through fasting
- through prayaschitta
- through vinay
- through swadhyay
- through meditation
- through long breathing
- through preksha

❖ There are two effects of awakening the psychic centre:

1. It alters the chemicals, controls anger and other emotions, and ends all addictions and bad habits.

2. Rays of purity emerging from the psychic centre unlock the door of inner bliss and knowledge.

17
Leshya: An Inspiration of Awakening

Leshya awakens the consciousness and obliterates delusion. The most important step is to be aware of your emotions, as they cause the mind to be unstable. Unless you awaken your higher consciousness through meditation, the emotional system cannot be refined. Therefore, transform your leshya and awaken your consciousness.

The process of meditation is the process of attaining consciousness of awareness by breaking through the delusions of physical life. Delusion or attachment is the foremost obstacle to attaining purity. Any process that deludes the consciousness is not a correct process of meditation. Only a perfect process of meditation can break delusion. Any substance or process that hides your consciousness can make your karma inert, and can make your kashay passive or dormant, but it does not destroy kashay.

When a person begins meditating, he can break through the delusions only if he reaches the field of emotions during the process of meditation after surpassing the field of karma. This means that it is necessary to reach the field of emotions to annihilate all delusions. Only then will your consciousness have access to the field of emotions. Material objects outside the physical self do not reach the level of emotions. You can stop your emotions at the physical level but the karma remains active. Therefore, you need to reach the root, the field of kashay. And the field of kashay can be treated or cured by understanding the mechanism of the field of leshya.

Lord Mahavir used two words to define violence and non-violence: *dravya* (physical) and *bhav* (psychical). If a person acts violently, speaks violently or thinks violently, this is dravya violence. But violence is not confined to the mind, body or speech. Conversely, if someone is non-violent in action, thought and words, this is not the complete world of non-violence. The two worlds – physical and psychical– flow into each other.

Kalsaukaric was a well-known slaughterer of animals in Lord Mahavir's time, around 2600 years ago. Every day he would kill 500 buffaloes. Bimbsar, the king of Magadha, wanted to transform him into a non-violent person. He began by having Kalsaukaric placed inside an empty well with no access to buffaloes. The king thought Kalsaukaric would lose interest in killing because he did not have access to animals. But it didn't have the desired effect. Forcibly preventing the act of killing did not make Kalsaukaric non-violent.

If a violent person becomes unconscious, he neither thinks nor acts violently while in this state. Does that make him non-violent? No, it doesn't, because when he regains consciousness he will be violent again. It doesn't matter if you make your body inactive or your mind unconscious, nothing is going to work unless your emotions are altered. No one is evil all the time. If someone does not think of violence and does not behave violently, it simply means that his karma is passive for the time being. We cannot say that his emotions have become positive.

Therefore we have to purify our emotions. When your emotional world is purified, no matter what situation you face, you will never hurt or even think of hurting another. Your negative qualities will be eradicated completely. As a matter of fact, you cannot rid yourself of delusion until the emotional system is purified. And until your delusion is eliminated, spiritual development is not possible.

Lord Mahavir achieved keval gyan and became omniscient.

His chief disciple, Indrabhuti Gautam, asked him, 'Bhante! What is *tattva*?'

'Tattva or real entity is that which originates, destroys and is permanent. Knowledge is permanent. When the impurity of knowledge is cleansed, pure knowledge emerges,' Lord Mahavir replied.

Gautam asked, 'Bhante! How did you attain keval gyan?'

Lord Mahavir replied, 'Gautam! I was completely aware. As I became aware, all delusion dissipated. After my awakening, everything was revealed with clarity. While I remained in delusion, my consciousness was hidden and dormant, and there was a veil of false reality. As soon as I was awakened the veil of delusion was removed. At this point keval gyan was achieved.'

Don't attempt to achieve the knowledge first; don't try to remove the obstacles right at the beginning of your meditative journey. First, try to end the delusion that attaches you to the external world. Delusion does not let you become aware. Try to awaken your own consciousness by doing away with delusion. Unless you awaken your higher consciousness through meditation, the emotional system cannot be refined. The first attempt to be made is to remove delusion.

Be aware. As your mind wanders, know, observe and be aware of its fickleness. If your hand is moving, be aware of the movement. It is important to be aware of these activities. But it is the most important to be aware of your emotions; be aware of the emotion that causes the mind to be fickle, to wander, and be unstable.

If you are aware of your mind, it can stabilize for some time but not for ever. If you are aware of the movement of your hand, it can stop moving for some time but not for ever. The energy that drives your mind and your movements is the power of emotions. Why does your mind produce negative and positive thoughts?

The function of the mind is to think. The quality of thoughts – evil or good – is not under the control of the mind. This is controlled by your emotions. A single emotion can produce millions of thoughts. If you are angry you might think a million thoughts, and along with these your entire body responds. Your breathing becomes fast, your voice shakes, your muscles are tensed. Conversely, if you are calm your thoughts are entirely different, because the emotion has changed. This is why it is more important to change your emotional pattern than your thoughts.

Constant awareness and vigilance are the ways to alter the emotional system. Be aware of your existence, awaken your consciousness. Watch the quality of your thoughts. Be an observer of your emotions. You don't need intoxicants to do so. Simply close your mind.

When your foundation is ready for awakening and you are beyond this physical system, certain questions arise: How do we conduct our daily affairs? How do we follow existing social behaviour? How will we react to others? If we have to consider the questions of hunger, mutual help, food and clothing when we are meditating, will it not create conflict and contradiction? Is this kind of meditation not impractical in the modern world? Will problems in life not become more critical? These are all obvious questions that are on everybody's mind.

When you are living life consumed with thoughts and are looking to move beyond them, this task appears daunting. When you go into a state of no thought, these queries do not arise. Once you move into the emotional field, these questions will not bother you. But if you are only thinking as an attempt to get into the field of emotions, questions will continue to bother you. It is difficult to explain these subtle concepts in words. As you start to meditate, everything will become crystal clear.

There are two worlds – the transcendental and the conventional. Your practical life demands many explanations. Practical systems work based on the conventional system. They do not interact with the transcendental system. You live in the conventional world. As long as you inhabit your body, you cannot ignore practical life. You cannot reject existing social disciplines and behave outside of them. As long as you reside in your body, you have to follow communal life. When you leave your body, these social obligations and behaviours will vanish.

So here is the answer to all your questions. I believe that one who practises purification of emotions does not stay away from his life; rather, he becomes more true and loyal to his duties. His social life becomes more successful. To understand this you will have to go deep into your inner self. You will have to understand what makes you unhappy or unsuccessful.

Two things make us unhappy – incident and thought. At different stages in life, you experience pain and at other times pleasure. Sometimes you experience the feeling of liking something or someone, and sometimes you register the feeling of dislike. Sometimes you feel a situation is favourable, sometimes unfavourable. The incident is not the issue here, but the thoughts about that incident make you see it as good or bad. How you react to that situation is what gives you pain or pleasure. The saying goes: 'There is nothing good or bad but thinking makes it so'. Some people are very sensitive. They stretch a small issue with their thoughts. If you have control over your senses and your imagination, an internal power is awakened and you can place your problems in perspective. As I said earlier, an incident is neither big nor small. It's your perception, your way of thinking that makes it big or small.

You will know the truth of the incident. You will try to overcome the problem. But do not get influenced by the incident. Let's understand it this way. Suppose a house is vandalized somewhere in your town. That is also an incident. You knew it but your mind did not get attached to it. So you did not get hurt. If you come to know that the victim is your friend, then you feel a little hurt. If such an incident happens to you, then your mind is strongly associated with this incident and your sensations and reaction become strong. Now analyse it. The incident is the same, but your reactions are different in each situation. When it happened to an unknown person, your mind or emotions were not connected. When it happened with you, then your mind and feelings were closely attached to the incident. So incidents are not responsible for your pain. Rather it is your connection to that incident that makes you feel hurt.

Sometimes people feel sympathy for an incident that happens far away. Sympathy is relative. Many times, the victims of such incidents do not feel pain but other people are more sympathetic. Strong and weak minds play important roles in this. A husband dies but the wife is strong enough to bear this mishap. She understands the truth of life. She accepts it bravely. However, her friends and family visit her and show their sympathy by shedding tears. She does not connect her mind with the incident so she is balanced. To have sympathy and to show sympathy are quite different. Many times we see that to show sympathy is not the solution.

People also create confusion by exaggerating meditation. They say meditation awakens consciousness and this can give you whatever you want. Such talk is fraudulent.

Once you get connected, you start adding your personal thoughts and views, which in turn multiplies your sentiments. These sentiments make you miserable. Therefore, keep your mind away from the incident and stay watchful.

The government of a country was planning mandatory service in the army for its citizens. The formal announcement had not yet been made. But one man became worried. He went to his friend and said, 'Are you not scared? Service in the army is going to be declared mandatory. I am very nervous. My brain is not working. Why aren't you frightened?'

His friend replied, 'Frightened? Of what? The declaration is not yet ratified. However, even when the announcement is made, who knows whether or not I will get called to serve in the army? Even if that happens, I don't know if they will send me to war. And if they do send me, I am not sure if I will be gunned down. Even if

I am gunned down and I die, what is the point of getting scared? For, who can have fear after death? Therefore, I don't allow my imagination to frighten me.'

An incident does not bother you directly. What bothers you is your reaction to it. By a chain of imaginary incidents you spin a web of pain and get trapped in it. It is the sensation rather than the incident that bothers you.

The question is: How can you control your imagination or thoughts? You can do this through meditation. In fact, someone who meditates can disconnect himself from the sensation of an incident. He is no longer physically connected to the incident. Don't assume that a person who meditates attains the power to stop incidents from occurring. What he does is stop the sensation caused by an incident.

Meditation helps you stay away from these sensations. It does not let you be emotionally sensitive. A person who meditates is not emotionally affected by incidents. The function of meditation is the segregation of the mind from the incident. The incident and the mind are both isolated. Will this negatively affect your social life? No. Meditation integrates a person into society. In fact, social life is negatively affected because of mental projection, doubts and sensations.

Many people come to me with family problems. A family is a group of people with diverse interests. Different interests lead to different thoughts, and conflicts might arise on any issue. The issue builds stress. It might be a small issue but it becomes big due to exaggerated thinking.

I believe that a big incident never caused a war. All great wars took place over small issues. I would like to illustrate an incident that occurred in ancient times. The Chakravarti king, Bharat, the son of Lord Rishabh, sent a message to his younger brother: 'Bahubali will have to obey me.'

King Bahubali replied, 'Bahubali does not obey anybody.'

If Bahubali was not ready to obey Bharat, why did it matter to Bharat? Both were ruling over their own kingdom. There was no need to compel anybody to follow Bharat. But the kings were ruled by their egos. When the ego is large, people want to extend their kingdom. Bharat's ego became so big that he was not ready to cool down. Consequently, a war was fought between the brothers for twelve years. It was the first great war in that era. And it was caused by ego. Therefore meditation is necessary to remove the ego and to solve conflicts.

WHY MEDITATE?

People are often wary of practising meditation because they are not sure of the process and result. They feel that they have to be isolated from their social life if they meditate. Let me remind you that a person who meditates only stops unnecessary formalities, not the necessary ones. Meditation always helps to build a healthy society. In fact, someone with a strong ego is more likely to get their society or nation into trouble. Such people never do meditation. I have never met a meditating person who is a troublemaker. So, I would suggest you remove any fear or doubt about meditation.

The first advantage of awakening the consciousness is healthy and decent behaviour.

The second benefit is that a person can live a happy life and die peacefully. Someone who does not awaken his self and does not meditate can neither have a happy life nor a peaceful death. If you do not have a peaceful death, you are likely to be unhappy in your next life. If you are strongly attached to your life, you cannot die peacefully. You will always be afraid of death and not be able to live your life to the fullest. If you long for life, and want to live for ever, you are running from death. And when it finally comes, you will find death painful.

Meditation helps you overcome these problems. You will not have attachments to your life, so you will not live in fear of death. Meditation helps you enter that stage of consciousness where life and death both appear coincidental. It is the aphorism of the contemplation of transitoriness: 'Life is a coincidence and death is a coincidence.'

The *Bhagawad Gita* says: 'As man wears new cloth by leaving the old; similarly, the soul abides in a new body and gives up the old body after death'. Why should one be afraid of death? Man knows about death. The fear of death resides inside. Rhetoric cannot get rid of fear – this can happen only by awakening the consciousness. What the *Bhagawad Gita* tells you is the truth but unless you bring this truth to your conscious level you cannot follow it. Lord Mahavir, Lord Buddha, Lord Krishna and Jesus Christ have all preached the same idea: 'Death is certain, do not fear it.' This truth cannot be understood until you achieve higher levels of consciousness through meditation.

A narrator was recounting the Mahabharata. When he finished he asked his audience what the essence of the great saga was. A devotee came forward and said, 'When Lord Krishna asked the Kauravas to give only five villages to the Pandavas and to rule over the rest of the land, Duryodhana said, "Lord Krishna! I am not going to give even a piece of land equal to the tip of a needle without war."

Until you awaken your power through meditation, no matter what you read, whether it is the best literature or scriptures, you will interpret it in a biased way. To understand Lord Mahavir, you have to pursue higher consciousness. It will take time to reach there but you should start your journey. If you want to understand Lord Buddha, Lord Rama, Lord Krishna, Jesus Christ or any other great souls, you have to develop your understanding by awakening your consciousness. You will have to attain the same pattern of thinking that the great souls had. Otherwise, you will misinterpret their teachings. Scholars who explained the teachings of the great souls without complete and true understanding did an injustice. They obscured the truth so that the reader cannot reach the true meaning contained in the original messages.

Only you can lead yourself to the truth. The words contained in the scripture cannot help you achieve this. How can experiences from thousands of years ago be understood only through words? To understand the experience, you need to have the same or similar experience. To understand the consciousness of the great souls you have to create the same consciousness. This is possible only through meditation.

If you want to practise meditation, if you want to develop spirituality, if you want to solve problems through spirituality, it is necessary to extend your consciousness. To do so is to disconnect the attachment of consciousness with matter. You will use objects but your consciousness will not get bonded to them. To eat food is the use of food but to like or dislike it is to get bonded. Those who meditate also eat food, drink water and save money. These are basic necessities that you cannot give up while you are alive. A spiritual person does not give up the physical world, but he does not get entangled in it either. This is the effect of higher consciousness. In this state, a sense of utility is there, but there is no attachment. Therefore, the root cause of the problem is solved.

It is true that for a successful life of humility and honesty, higher consciousness is necessary. For inner development and the awakening of power, to remove the obstacles to knowledge, the awakening of consciousness is necessary. To make your life happy, peaceful and humble, you need to develop higher consciousness.

If you want to practise meditation, overcome your doubts and don't get stuck on irrational questions. Dive into deep introspection, give importance to experience and realize the truth. Don't depend on other people. Your maxim is *Appana sachcha-mesejja*, search for truth by yourself; don't just believe what others tell you. When you realize the need to seek the truth yourself, when you experience the truth through meditation, your delusion and outer problems will be over and you will be able to live a successful and happy life.

While getting into deep meditation some practitioners start laughing or crying. They are not even conscious of their outbursts. Is this spirituality?

Only when meditation is accompanied by delusion do such incidents take place. It does not happen in the state of awareness. I believe that such things happen in hypnotism. Through hypnotism one can be made to laugh or cry, for these are subtle instincts, present in all human beings. Sometimes it gets manifested through experiments. But the primary purpose of meditation is to awaken the consciousness so it is not necessary to bring these emotions out in this way. It is true that the energy of these instincts needs to be expelled. But it is not necessary that the energy of laughter be released through laughing, the energy of crying through tears, or the energy of sex through sexual pleasure.

There are two techniques: delusion and awakening. If you are working with the technique of awakening, you do not need to laugh or cry. Thousands of spiritual practitioners have practised meditation in search of truth; they have realized the truth through awakening. Nowhere does it say that they ever laughed or cried. To laugh and to cry are the enjoyment of the instincts while the purpose of awakening is to weaken the instinct and thereby shed off the energy.

What is the difference between bhav and bhavana?

Bhav is an emotional system within us at the subtle level and bhavana is the manifestation of emotions at the gross level, in our words, thoughts and actions.

The unconsciousness or delusion in some plants is at its peak. They die and are reborn in the same form in an endlesss cycle. Is there any way of upgrading these souls?

When an intense delusion is present, there is no way of achieving higher consciousness. When this delusion is diluted, the soul can move forward. There are two factors that can dilute the delusion – time and practice. The former is natural and the latter is acquired. Time itself becomes a firm factor for breaking this intense unconsciousness. Certain things depend on time. We grow with time. A child does not become a youth after only five years. It takes time. Similarly, as time progresses, the delusion of such plants begins to dissipate. The moment delusion is weakened, the consciousness is uplifted and their souls are promoted to take birth at other places in other forms.

ESSENCE

❖ Omniscient knowledge means inner awareness.

❖ Delusion is a state of unawareness, which strengthens your karma and makes you more materialistic.

❖ Deluded consciousness makes a person more covetous. In this mindset, he cannot have a peaceful death. He is always afraid of death, which adversely affects his ability to live a good life.

❖ The awakening of consciousness affects both karma and emotions.

❖ The only way to awaken the consciousness is to be aware of yourself. Close your mind. This means maintaining a thoughtless state of mind and constant realization of the self.

❖ Meditation does not segregate you from the material world; instead it helps you identify worldly truths and facts.

In this state:

❖ Matter is used but there is no attachments to it.

❖ Matter becomes a utility, not the cause of pleasure and pain.

❖ The power of tolerance is developed. You are not swayed by any incident.

❖ Unaffectedness or stability of the consciousness is realized.

❖ Conventional and transcendental lives move alongside each other.

❖ Man lives and dies peacefully.

❖ The aura gets purified and the right perspective is developed.

Appendix 1

AURA AND COLOUR

❖ Sound and colour are both states of vibrations. They can be converted to each other. There are seven colours and seven types of sound. They all affect our body. Colour affects us at the physical, mental, emotional and spiritual levels.

❖ Colour is negative while light is positive in nature.

❖ The system of endocrine glands in physiology and the system of psychic centres in preksha dhyan are both the same. Each endocrine gland has its own hue and the gland is activated through the corresponding colour.

❖ Colour is a fraction of light. It is the forty-ninth vibration of light. The range of colours seen in visible light are different vibrations of light. The number of vibrations for each colour is constant. Red vibrates 4.3×10^{14} times in a second while the frequency of violet is 7.3×10^{14} Hz.

❖ Colour is a holistic therapy for healing because it corrects the imbalance of the body. Balance of colour gives you life while imbalance brings death. In fact, colour is the real food of the body. The food man ingests when eating vegetables is nothing but condensed colour.

- ✣ Colour can make your body active and sluggish as well.
- ✣ Right knowledge and the correct use of colour can increase your lifespan. Colour reveals things about you. Know thyself as your colour speaks.
- ✣ When a child is born, he comes with a violet colour. Its wave length is the shortest one. As he grows, the continuity of vibrations gets disturbed, the frequency decreases and wave length increases. When it reaches the last point of red, he dies.
- ✣ All living beings have some colour.
- ✣ If you practise meditation at the forty-ninth vibration of blue it helps cure disease. If a person goes beyond the forty-ninth vibration he dies.
- ✣ Eye diseases can be depicted by the colour of eyes. There are 72 eye ailments.

COLOURS SPEAK

Red

Red is the element of fire. It activates the blood and nervous system. It also activates the motor nerves to stimulate muscle contraction. The activities of all five sense organs depend on this colour. Red motivates the cerebral hemispheres and helps control the cerebra-spinal chemicals. Red produces heat in the body and directs power within the body. These rays are beneficial for the liver and muscles. Moreover, red keeps the right hemisphere of our brain active. The waves of red break up the alkaline substance in the body. With this colour, the body undergoes the process of ionization. These ions are the carrier of the electro-magnetic power. Without it the body can never take everything it needs from the outside.

According to psychology, red is good for health. It is the colour of resistance. But excess of this colour can create fever and laziness.

Yellow

Yellow activates the motor nerves and strengthens the muscles. It is not an independent colour. It is a mixture of red and green and contains the qualities of both these colours. Yellow can make dead cells come alive and become active. Yellow is a positive electro-magnetic energy, that also strengthens the brain and nervous system.

Yellow is the colour of intelligence and faith. It removes mental weakness and dejection. Yellow is also the symbol of cheerfulness and happiness.

Orange

Orange is a mixture of yellow and red but it is more aggressive and warm than both colours. It is the colour of heat, fire, resolution and material power. It helps in breathing and keeps the thyroid gland active. The vibration of this colour strengthens the lungs. It increases the secretion of milk in women. It helps the pancreas stay healthy and also aids in the circulation of bile.

Orange also connects physical strength with mental qualities. It forces the flow of energy from the spleen and pancreas. It is the indicator of thoughts and imagination. It helps maintain love, happiness and imagination.

Green

Green is the colour of nitrogen gas. It is useful in maintaining mental peace and physical health. It strengthens the muscles, bones and cells and reduces blood pressure. It activates the pituitary glands and builds muscles and tissues. This colour works like an antiseptic but it also stimulates sensual desires. It has positive effects in the beginning but later becomes harmful.

Green is the symbol of power, youth, experience, creativity, hope and new life. But it is also the symbol of jealousy, hate and superstition.

Blue

Blue works like a tonic for blood. It is the colour of empowerment, coolness, electricity and contraction. It increases blood pressure and contracts the nerves. When blood is excessively active and hot, blue is used to bring it to the normal state. It soothes the stimulations of the nervous system.

Blue is the most helpful in emotional situations. It is the symbol of meditation and spiritual development. It keeps our mind calm and purifies the *visuddhi kendra* (centre of purity). It removes selfishness and makes a person social and comfortable with their surroundings. Blue is the indicator of truth, dedication, peace, honesty and insight.

It also has certain negative effects. The shower of blue rays, even for ten minutes, makes a person tired. Blue outfits and blue furniture cause fatigue, but if it is mixed with another colour it does not dominate.

Indigo

Indigo makes the thyroid gland inactive and stimulates the parathyroid gland. It strengthens muscle power, purifies the blood and calms breathing.

This colour controls the centre of knowledge (on top of the head) and the inner bioelectric power of microbodies. It influences the power of vision, hearing and smell at physical, emotional and spiritual levels.

Violet

It is the colour of fostering the frontal lobe of the brain. It affects bile and weakens the motor nerves. It helps in purifying blood and developing bones.

Violet is very useful for getting rid of violent madness. It is an inspirational colour and helps control hyper appetite. It controls the centre of health, which is the navel. Some scholars believe that in violet light one can get into a meditative state ten times faster. If violet light is passed through an uncoated mirror, the power of meditation is developed.

Lemon

Lemon colour stimulates the brain. The thymus gland has an element, uranium, that is responsible for physical growth. When the uranium is depleted the growth stops. This lemon colour helps the thymus gland stay active. It has the qualities of both yellow and green.

PSYCHIC CENTRES AND COLOUR

Shakti Kendra (Mooladhar Chakra)

It is yellow in colour and consists of the earth element. Sushumna Nadi and Kundalini both originate here.

Swasthya Kendra (Swadhisthan Chakra)

Its colour is orange and it consists of the water element. This centre is responsible for making the aura.

It attracts pure vital energy along with oxygen from the sun's ultraviolet rays. This vital energy is then transmitted to the entire body by means of nerves. The used and superfluous energy of vital energy emerge through the skin, which is known as aura. Every living being is endowed with an aura but only some have a halo.

Taijas Kendra (Manipur Chakra)

It is red and the element is fire.

Anand Kendra (Anahat Chakra)

Violet is its colour and air is the element.

Vishuddhi Kendra (Vishuddha Chakra)

It is purple and the element is ether.

Darshan Kendra (Agna Chakra)

It is blue. It is the place where Ida nadi, Pingala nadi and Sushumna nadi meet. The colour of Ida is indigo, the colour of Pingala is red and the colour of Sushumna is deep red.

Gyan Kendra (Sahsrar Chakra)

It is green in colour. When this centre is active all colours are present.

PSYCHIC CENTRES AND THEIR LOCATION

	Chaitanya Kendra	Psychic centres	Analogous Endocrine glands (Internal location)	Physical Location
1	Gyan Kendra	Centre of knowledge	Cerebral cortex	Top of the head
2	Shanti Kendra	Centre of enlightenment	Hypothalamus	Front part of the head
3	Jyoti Kendra	Centre of peace	Pineal	Centre of forehead
4	Darshan Kendra	Centre of intuition	Pituitary	Middle of the eyebrows
5	Apramad Kendra	Centre of vigilence	Sense organ of hearing	Ears
6	Chakshusha Kendra	Centre of vision	Sense organ of sight	Eyes
7	Pran Kendra	Centre of vital energy	Sense organ of smell	Nose (tip)

8	Brahm Kendra	Centre of celibacy	Sense organ of taste	Tongue (tip)
9	Vishuddhi Kendra	Centre of purity	Thyroid, Parathyroid	Adam's apple, throat
10	Anand Kendra	Centre of bliss	Thymus	Near the heart
11	Taijas Kendra	Centre of bioelectricity	Adrenal, pancreas, Islets of Langerhans	Navel
12	Swasthya Kendra	Centre of health	Gonads	Lower abdomen
13	Shakti Kendra	Centre of energy	Gonads	Bottom of the spinal cord

Appendix 2

PRACTICAL EXERCISES OF PREKSHA MEDITATION

PREKSHA MEDITATION TO OVERCOME ANGER

Anger is the most apparent negative emotion in humans. Anger causes a loss of self-monitoring capacity and the right perception. Therefore, an angry person can easily make a mistake. Anger affects our health and relationships badly. For happiness and harmony, managing anger is the first need.

Perception of bright white colour at the Centre of Enlightenment:

1. Sit in a comfortable posture – lotus, prayer posture or simple cross-leg posture.
2. *Gyan mudra:* Put your hands on your knees; palms turned up. Touch the tip of your index finger to the tip of your thumb. Let your other fingers remain straight.
3. Close your eyes softly.

4. *Mahapran dhwani*: 9 times. To practice Mahapran dhwani, focus on your brain. Breathe in through your nostrils then, while exhaling, make a resonant humming sound like a buzzing bee.

5. Relax your body from the head to the toes. Loosen your muscles.

6. Slow your breathing. Inhale white air.

7. Concentrate on the Centre of Enlightenment, located at the central point of your forehead.

8. Allow your mind to penetrate the Centre and perceive the bright white colour there. Visualize the bright white light of the full moon or snow at the Centre of Enlightenment and spreading throughout the forehead.

9. Repeat the following sentences first loudly (nine times) and then mentally (nine times):
    - ✤ I am not anger. Anger is not my nature.
    - ✤ To forgive is the true nature of the consciousness.

10. With deep concentration say the following autosuggestions:
    - ✤ Anger is going away. Forgiveness is developing.
    - ✤ Anger is not good for my health, relations and peaceful life.
    - ✤ I will stay balanced and positive.
    - ✤ I am becoming cool, calm and quiet in any adverse situation.

11. Keep repeating the sentences mentally for a while and experience yourself as free from anger.

12. Experience complete tranquility, complete mental peace and bliss.

13. Conclude the meditation by doing mahapran dhwani 3 times.

PREKSHA MEDITATION TO CONTROL LUST

Sexual impulses are obstacles to personal spiritual growth and to a healthy society. Unsatisfied urges beget anger, deceit, enmity and other negative emotions. Therefore, for a peaceful life and society one must have control over such urges.

Perception of bright blue colour at the Centre of Purity:

1. Steps 1 to 5 are the same as the former.
2. With your mind's eye visualize everything around you, including the air, as being, coloured bright blue like a peacock's neck.
3. Take a deep breath and as you slowly inhale, visualize that you are breathing bright blue air. Repeat the breathing exercise several times, to inhaling bright blue air each time.
4. Now concentrate on the Centre of Purity, located at the central point of the throat and try to visualize bright blue colour over there.
5. Visualize and experience the blue radiations spreading in the psychic centre covering the entire area up to the back. (If the light does not appear or vanishes after appearing, do not get disappointed.) Intensify your effort for sustained visualization.
6. Now imagine that the particles or radiations of bright blue light are coming out of the Centre of Purity and spreading all around, permeating the whole body and the aura. Practise sustained visualization with deep concentration.
7. Repeat the following sentences first loudly (nine times) and then mentally (nine times):
    ❖ Lust is not my nature.
    ❖ My true nature is celibacy.
8. Now practise autosuggestion on yourself:
    ❖ Sexual impulses decrease my energy level.
    ❖ To develop the level of vital energy and purity I need to control the sexual impulses.
    ❖ My sexual impulses are getting under my conscious control.
    ❖ My emotions are getting purified.
9. Keep repeating the sentences mentally for a while and experience freedom from lust.
10. Conclude the meditation with 3 repetitions of mahapran dhwani.

PREKSHA MEDITATION TO DEVELOP PATIENCE

Patience is a positive virtue indicating a voluntary self-control while waiting. It helps to stay free from anxiety. In a general way it shows tolerance for other people's shortcomings, and an ability to remain unperturbed by others' inefficiency and to bear annoying situations without becoming upset. It is a very much desired virtue for a peaceful life as well as social harmony.

Perception of bright yellow colour at the Centre of Vital Energy:

1. Steps 1 to 5 are same as the first. With your mind's eye visualize that everything around you, including the air is coloured bright yellow like a sunflower.

2. Take a deep breath and as you slowly inhale, visualize that you are breathing bright yellow air. Repeat the breathing exercise several times, inhaling bright yellow air each time.

3. Now focus on the Centre of Vital Energy, located at the tip of your nose and try to visualize bright yellow colour over there.

4. Repeat the following sentences first loudly (nine times) and then mentally (nine times):

    ✤ I will develop my capacity to confront any situation with patience.

    ✤ I will not lose patience and be overwhelmed by any adversity.

5. Now practise autosuggestion on yourself:

    ✤ One who is impatient and does not wait for the opportune moment, becomes over-agitated.

    ✤ Over-agitation results in mental ineffectiveness.

    ✤ This drastically reduces the power of memory and concentration.

    ✤ To preserve these, it is essential to cultivate the virtue of patience.

    ✤ My patience is developing.

6. Keep repeating the sentences mentally for a while so that you feel that you are capable of being patient.
7. Conclude the meditation with 3 repetitions of mahapran dhwani.

PREKSHA MEDITATION TO DEVELOP HONESTY

Honesty is an estimable and desirable inner virtue. Honesty refers to a facet of moral character and denotes positive attributes such as integrity, truthfulness, and straightforwardness along with the absence of lying, cheating or theft. Honesty comes from the absence of temptation.

Perception of bright yellow colour at the Centre of Enlightenment:

1. Step 1 to 5 are same as the first.
2. With your mind's eye visualize that everything around you, including the air, is coloured bright yellow like a sunflower.
3. Take a deep breath and as you slowly inhale, visualize that you are breathing bright yellow air. Repeat the breathing exercise several times, each time inhaling bright yellow air.
4. Focus your full attention on the Centre of Enlightenment and recite the following sentences first loudly (nine times) and then mentally (nine times):
   ❖ My will-power is increasing.
   ❖ My inherent faith in honesty is getting reinforced.
5. Visualize and experience that the yellow radiations are spreading in the psychic centre covering the entire area. (If the light does not appear or comes and goes, do not get disappointed.) Intensify your effort for sustained visualization.
6. Now visualize that the particles or radiations of bright yellow light are coming out from the Centre of Enlightenment and spreading all around, permeating the whole body and the aura.
7. Now use the method of autosuggestion:

- ✤ Dishonesty is an undesirable evil attitude.
- ✤ A dishonest man never succeeds in the long run.
- ✤ Honesty builds trust and relations.
- ✤ I resolve that nothing would ever make me dishonest; my behaviour will always be guided by my rational mind and not by my impulses.

8. Keep repeating the sentences mentally for some time and experience that you are full of patience.
9. Conclude the meditation with 3 repetitions of mahapran dhwani.

PREKSHA MEDITATION TO MANAGE THE DESIRES (GREED)

Greed is an insatiable desire for food, money, power or material possessions. A greedy person would not hesitate to use unethical means to fulfill his desire and greed or uncontrolled desires can lead a man to violence. To promote social health, one must make a moral effort to practice freedom from greed by developing self-restraint.

Perception of bright blue colour at the Centre of Celibacy:

1. Steps 1 to 5 are the same as the first.
2. Visualize that everything around you, including the air, is coloured bright blue like a peacock's neck.
3. Take a deep breath and as you slowly inhale, visualize that you are breathing bright blue air. Repeat the breathing exercise several times, inhaling bright blue air each time.
4. Now focus on the Centre of Celibacy, located at the tip of the tongue and try to visualize bright blue colour over there. Recite the following sentences first loudly (nine times) and then mentally (nine times):
   - ✤ I am becoming free from the instinct of greed.
   - ✤ My self-restraint and satisfaction are developing.
5. Now visualize that the particles or radiations of bright blue light are coming out of the Centre of Celibacy and spreading all around,

permeating the whole body and the aura. Practise sustained visualization with deep concentration.

6. Now practise autosuggestion on yourself:
    ✤ Greed is an evil instinct of life.
    ✤ It produces desire and selfishness.
    ✤ It compels one to hoard material possessions.
    ✤ The more I get the more stressed I am.
    ✤ Therefore I must develop satisfaction.

8. Keep repeating the sentences mentally for a while and experience that you are content and free of cravings.

9. Conclude the meditation with repetitions of mahapran dhwani.

Glossary

arta dhyan	to focus on or think about separation from the favorable and the association with the unfavorable object, situation or person
adhyavasay	the field of conscious vibration. When pure conscious vibrations come across the field of kashay they become impure. After coming out of this field the vibrations form a field. This is *adhyavasay*. When your conscious energy goes up to *adhyavasay*, your body is left behind. There is no connection between the physical body and *adhyavasay*
anupreksha	to reflect upon what is eternal, true and real. To affect attitudinal change by the process of autosuggestion and repeated recitation is also known as *anupreksha*
apay vichay	reflection on the flaw of the negative instincts
apramatta	complete awareness of the self
asan	physical exercise or yoga
bhav leshya	the state of the soul due to *dravya leshya*
bhavana	frequent and prolonged repetition of an idea

chitta	a conscious ray, which works with our body and mind at the gross level. The *chitta* is incorporeal in nature. So, it does not have any colour or physical properties
dravya leshya	the atoms that make the *leshya*
kapot leshya	the grey aural colouration; one of the inauspicious or negative *leshya*
karma	the special type of material aggregate that is attracted to the soul on account of its activity and ultimately get bound to it. They give their effect as pain or pleasure and are the cause of transmigration (birth and death)
kashay	intemperance of the nature of attachment and hatred; literally means passion
kayotsarg	relaxation of body with awareness of the self
kevali	Means omniscient ; the soul who has attained pure, perfect and crystallized knowledge through which he can know all the substances of the world with all the modes of all three periods of time (present, past and future). It is the true and intrinsic nature of the soul and is attained on total elimination of the knowledge veiling karma
krishn leshya	the black aural colouration; the worst of the three inauspicious or negative *leshya*
Laxmi	the goddess of wealth accepted in Indian culture
leshya	it is an aural colouration. It is a transformation of the soul or consciousness on account of the karma attracted through the activity of mind, body and vocal. Depending on the activity, the soul attracts the analogous colour of karma. This colourful transformation is known as *leshya*
mahavrati	one who follows the five great vows. They are: non-violence, truth, not stealing, celibacy and non-possessiveness. A Jain ascetic follows these vows completely his whole life
mithyadrishti	the state of the soul possessed with perverted or false belief of the truth

neel leshya	the blue aural colouration, the middle quality of the inauspicious or negative leshya
nirjara	the shedding of karma and thereby purification of the soul
Nirvan	*nirvan* or emancipation means the establishment of the soul in its own nature on account of the destruction of all its karma. It is the purest state of the soul. There is no incarnation of such liberated souls.
padm	the yellow aural colouration; the middle quality of auspicious or positive *leshya*
pranayam	to regulate the breath through breathing exercise
pratikraman	in Jainism a way to self analysis
pratisanlinta	it means withdrawal of the sense organs and the like from the external objects
pratyakhyan	a vow or resolution to develop purity
Preksha	to see the self profoundly or deeply without attraction or revulsion.
pudgal	the physical entity, which can be in the form of matter, atom, aggregates or energy. *Pudgal* or matter has four characteristics – touch, taste, odor and colour
raudra dhyan	to focus on preserving the worldly things, violence, falsehood and stealing
samyak-drishti	the state of the soul possessed of firm conviction in the integrity of the truth
shukla	the white aural colouration; the best quality of auspicious or positive *leshya*
taijas sharir	a luminous body composed of the luminous atoms. It makes possible the supernatural power of thermoluminescene, effulgence and digestion.
tejo	the red aural colouration; the lowest quality of auspicious or positive *leshya*

vipak vichay	analysis on the consequences of karma
veetragi	one who is free from *rag* (attachment) and *dvesh* (aversion)
vrati	one who takes a resolution or vow that stops the accumulation of karma
vyutsarg	detachment from the body

About the Author

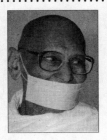

Acharya Mahapragya was the tenth Acharya of the Jain Swetambar Terapanth sect and one of the most widely respected Jain thinkers of the world. Born in 1920 in a village in Rajasthan, he became a monk at the age of ten. He got his education under the guidance of Acharya Shree Tulsi, who launched the Anuvrat movement in 1949 to rid the world of violence and hatred and free religion from sectarianism.

A multidimensional personality and a renowned scholar of Indian and Western philosophy and religion, Acharya Mahapragya traversed more than 100,000 km on foot over his lifetime and visited 10,000 villages to spread the message of non-violence. To this purpose he embarked on an Ahimsa Yatra in 2001. He was honoured with the Communal Harmony Award in 2004 for his contribution in this field. He recently passed away at the age of eighty-nine.

He is the author of numerous books, including *The Happy and Harmonious Family* (HarperCollins, 2009) and *The Family and the Nation* with A.P.J. Abdul Kalam (HarperCollins, 2008).